- What is abnormal sex?
- Do particular foods or drugs stimulate the sex drive?
- How long can sperm live?
- Do boys have a different interest in sex from girls?
- What does the expression "female trouble" mean?
- What is a wet dream?

With this book you won't have to be afraid of the questions—or the answers.

WARDELL B. POMEROY received the A.B. degree and M.A. degree in psychology from Indiana University, and the Ph.D. degree from Columbia University. As research associate at the Institute for Sex Research, he was co-author with the late Alfred Kinsey of *Sexual Behavior in the Human Male* and *Sexual Behavior in the Human Female*. He is academic dean emeritus at the Institute for Advanced Study of Human Sexuality in San Francisco, where he lives with his family.

GIRLS AND SEX

THIRD·EDITION

by
Wardell B. Pomeroy, Ph.D.

Co-author of the Kinsey Report
and author of *Boys and Sex*

Delacorte Press and Laurel-Leaf Books
Published by
Dell Publishing
a division of
Bantam Doubleday Dell Publishing Group, Inc.
666 Fifth Avenue
New York, New York 10103

RL: 10.0

Library of Congress Cataloging in Publication Data

Pomeroy, Wardell Baxter.
    Girls and sex / by Wardell B. Pomeroy.—3rd rev. ed.
        p.   cm.
    Includes bibliographical references.
    Summary: Discusses the physical, emotional, and ethical aspects of sex
including such topics as dating, petting, intercourse and its consequences,
lesbianism, and other related topics.
    ISBN 0-385-30251-7 (hc)   ISBN 0-440-20812-2 (pbk)
    1. Sex instruction for girls.   2. Sexual ethics—Juvenile literature.
[1. Sex instruction for girls.   2. Sexual ethics.]
    I. Title.
HQ51.P6   1991
306.7'0835'2—dc20   90-3144
                                                            CIP
Manufactured in the United States of America   AC

February 1991

10 9 8 7 6 5 4 3

RAD

*This book is fondly dedicated
to my wife, Martha*

Contents

Preface to the Third Edition

It's been a decade since the second edition of this book was published. In the preface I noted the "great social change in the area of human sexuality" since the first edition, in 1969. It was an understandable development, since the full effect of the social revolution of the sixties was becoming evident in the decade of the seventies.

But in the decade since 1981, we have had a national swing to conservatism in many respects; consequently it's not easy to understand why, paradoxically, the sexual scene has changed so much again that a new and revised edition seems necessary. Those who have had to deal with young children—teachers and parents—can testify, however, that while conservatism may have made considerable progress among older adults, its effect on the younger generation has been minimal, at least as far as sex is concerned. Both in vocabulary and in sexual behavior, these youngsters are growing up in a different world than their older brothers and sisters knew, for reasons too complex to go into here.

While both sexes have been affected by the change, girls have felt it more than boys, as the result of new freedoms stemming from the women's movement toward equal rights and responsibilities, as well as equal jobs and pay. The word "girls" itself has been under attack, but I've used it in the book's title and elsewhere because no one would describe the age group for which it's intended as composed of women.

All these changes are reflected in this revision, in one way or another. Vocabulary has been brought up to date and new attitudes examined carefully, in an attempt to resolve some of the confusion and difficulties that beset early adolescents and preteens in a different and often difficult sexual world.

I have drawn not only on the resources and professional colleagues cited in the second edition but on those acquired in the intervening decade. To all of these individuals I extend my renewed gratitude and thanks. I have also had the collaboration of John Tebbel, who has worked with me on all my books from the beginning. He has not only done the actual writing but has helped to clarify my thoughts.

I want also to offer renewed thanks to my wife,

Martha, to whom this book is dedicated. Once more she has been a constant source of support in the preparation of this revision, as she has been in earlier editions of the book, and of *Boys and Sex* as well.

GIRLS AND SEX

Introduction

Girls are growing up today in a sexual world entirely different from the one their parents knew, and radically different again from what their grandparents experienced. Never in the history of our country have sexual customs and behavior changed so radically in so short a time, and never has there been so much public acceptance of human sexuality. We see it in motion pictures and television, in books and magazines. Language and situations that were comparatively rare ten years ago are commonplace now.

All this has made it even more difficult for parents to talk to their growing daughters (and sons) about sex. You may feel that you know more about sex than your parents, and in some cases you may be right. Parents still rely pretty much on school, church, and friends to convey needed information. But since the information is so easily available from the media, a sort of mass learning process goes on. The trouble is, these media displays of sex don't provide you with all the information, by any means. So it's possible to see and read about a lot of sexual situations without really understanding what they're all about. It's easy to believe you know more about sex than you actually do.

You need that information now more than ever, in a world where AIDS has suddenly made sexual behavior a national fear as well as a personal pleasure. You and your friends are growing up more rapidly these days than your parents did. When I first wrote this book, twenty years ago, not many girls younger than thirteen would have read it. Now I think of girls who are no more than ten, eleven, or twelve as part of my audience. You're already reading books written for your age group by such very popular writers as Judy Blume, containing quite explicit sexual situations. Good as they may be, however, such books are long on entertainment and short on real information. Sex may not be the mystery it once was, never to be revealed until you were grown up, but the same old problems and the same old areas of misinformation seem to crop up just the same.

I'm sure many of you think your parents don't understand you, but whether that's true or not, I hope *you'll* try to understand your parents in sexual matters. They're likely to believe girls are growing up too fast, and they hate to lose the little girl they cuddled when she was five or six. What's going on today alarms and confuses them. So there's uneasiness on both sides about sex, and neither side really wants to talk about it. "Oh, Mother!" is still the common response when any attempt is made. That's meant to end the conversation.

If there's such a gulf between you and your parents, I'm hoping this book will help both of you to bridge it, because this particular gulf is really unnecessary. Both should be able to talk naturally about something that's the most natural thing in the world and the most common human activity. You and your friends have a sexual freedom today that no previous generation enjoyed, but it's possible that many of you don't quite know what to do with it. Parents are worried that you'll do the wrong thing. Yet the guidelines are simple enough, once you have the information you need. It's mostly a matter of knowledge and common sense.

Forget the "sexual revolution" we've all heard so much about. Parents who talk about "permissiveness" are repeating what has been said in one way or another for thousands of years. An Egyptian papyrus of 1700 B.C. tells us that the elders of an Egyptian city were convinced the young people of their community were going to the dogs, as the old saying goes. They complained about the disregard for authority by the young, and they were especially annoyed because young boys were driving their chariots recklessly over the landscape, without regard for life or limb. As for the girls, the elders were horrified that they were shamelessly painting their lips with henna.

But it's only partly true that things haven't changed

since then. A steady process of evolution has gone on, and today we're in a major new stage of this process because, perhaps for the first time in human history, the male view of women no longer predominates. Women have begun to play a role in society that they were always denied before, with only a relative few determined exceptions. Women now make up nearly half the work force, and the proportion is growing. They now have choices: a career in business or the professions, a traditional career as a housewife and raiser of children, or a combination of both—"having it all," as we say. This freedom has produced its own problems, but there is no doubt that we're seeing one of the greatest social changes in history.

As equality of the sexes becomes a social reality, we've seen a remarkable change in the old double standard about sex, although it certainly hasn't disappeared, by any means. My former colleague, Dr. Kinsey, was first to recognize that women have the same biological response as men. Today more and more women have begun to understand their own sexuality a great deal better, to be more assertive about it, and to insist that they are sexual beings as much as men, with needs and desires of their own. The sexes are different in some ways in their psychological responses, but that's a matter we'll take up later.

In spite of the great change, there's one kind of sexual activity that remains divisive in some respects, and that's premarital intercourse. This is surprising, too, since it's now commonplace for people to live together before they're married, or at least to have regular sexual intercourse. People also accept the fact that intercourse may begin much earlier than it used to. Older women no longer regard marriage as inevitable or absolutely required by society. But even though they know all these things go on, most parents don't want them happening to their own daughters. If you don't think so, just imagine the reaction if you should say to your mother, "Mom, I'm sleeping with Joe these days, and it's really a lot of fun." It's still common to hear mothers of college-age girls saying, "Well, I know she's living with him off campus, but if she brings him home, she can't sleep with him—not under *my* roof."

As for girls of high school age and under, not only does the law forbid it, but most parents don't approve of premarital intercourse when they suspect it's occurring. Some parents, of course, are more strict than others in trying to prevent it.

Premarital intercourse, however, has been creeping up on us (as an acceptable activity) for the past fifty years. It flourished at the upper social levels, where money made practically any kind of behavior possible and sophistication accepted it. But it was also even more common at lower levels, then and now. Until it became possible to get contraceptives easily, we could measure its advance by the rise in teen-age pregnancies. That teen-age intercourse can also generate its own problems is evident in the high suicide rate among teens, where it's a factor in a surprising number of cases and adds to adolescent despair over the state of the world and their own lives.

The key word is still "acceptance." It's hard to realize that the word "syphilis," much less any really sexual word, did not appear in an American newspaper until 1932, and it was four years later before the word was uttered on the radio. The word "masturbation" wasn't seen in a newspaper in this country until 1948, and homosexuality was not discussed in the mass media until about 1960. Now it's difficult to find newspapers, books, magazines, or plays that *don't* deal with these and other sexual subjects in one way or another, openly and more or less freely, although often with considerable ignorance.

Does all this mean there's been an equal change in overt sexual *behavior*? Probably not. It simply means there's been a change in the open *discussion* of sex. We're a very big country now, racing on toward the 250 million mark, and that means there are more people engaging in sexual behavior of all sorts, and that may lead people to the incorrect conclusion that there's an increase in sexual activity.

Another change we've seen is in the status of pornography, once condemned by law as well as by most people. It's still condemned by some feminists who regard it as a degrading attack on women, and by those in religious groups, and by others. But the Supreme Court, after years of trying to define it with no success, has been vague enough in its recent decisions so that almost anything can now be printed, or seen in stationary and moving images, except for scenes involving children. We're far from seeing the last of this argument, however. The attempt to censor has been going on since the early days of the country, and it shows no sign of diminishing. Strong forces want a return to the old restrictions, but for now we still have the freedom that the First Amendment has guaranteed all along.

But if our society is really heading toward still more liberal attitudes about sex, and the present conservative rollback proves to be temporary, a question arises—and it arises especially among parents: What's the effect going to be? You've probably heard older people say that all this sexual freedom means the end of civilization, and no doubt they'll point to the fall of the Roman Empire, even though the sexual habits of the Romans had little if anything to do with the collapse of their world.

On the other hand, it's equally true that even greater sexual freedom would not mean a new era of universal happiness and self-fulfillment. That wouldn't happen, nor would it decrease such things as racial tensions and war, improve the lot of the poor, or lead us directly to healthier lives. Sex, freedom or not, is only a part of our lives, only a part of the fabric of civilization. It isn't even the primary moving force in human experience. Encouraging it or discouraging it won't solve our problems. Sexual experience is more an effect than a cause. That's not to say that sexual intercourse itself isn't a deeply emotional and loving experience, at its best, but it can also be an aggressive and hostile act, or no more than a casual toss on the mattress, without meaning. The same thing can be said for any other kind of sexual behavior.

The fact is—and most people find this hard to believe—we really don't know as much as we think we do about sex. We're still in the Dark Ages as far as solid research on sexual behavior is concerned. Fewer than a hundred research projects in this field can be said to be adequate and important. No other area of human behavior remains so unexplored.

Because we don't know enough, however, doesn't mean that boys and girls, as well as their parents, can avoid the responsibility to learn as much as they can about sex and to make as much sense out of it as possible. Parents, especially, ought to stop viewing sexual behavior through the distorted lens of the prejudices and fears they grew up with. They should see it as part of a changing world. Their children are going to grow up in this world and will have to learn how to deal with sex in a way that will give them as much happiness as possible.

Daughters have a particularly hard time of trying to make their parents see things from that point of view. Parents, grandparents, and ancestors back through the generations have always believed girls had to be protected. Even parents who talk easily about how much things have changed often don't seem to think it applies to the behavior of their young daughters.

Things *do* change slowly. Parents are still asking, "How can I talk to my daughter about sex?" They seem to think that if such talks are possible, it's solely a matter between mother and daughter. If the problem rises at all, it happens when a girl is seen to be growing up, and that's happening at an earlier age these days.

What was once fourteen-year-old "growing up" often begins now at eleven, on occasion even earlier. The sure sign is when a girl wants to go out with a boy for the first time.

When parents ask me how to handle this situation, I tell them they're asking it several years too late. They've been communicating with their daughter about sex from the time she was old enough to understand anything, I say. *Not* talking with her about sex is sex education in itself. In that case, she will understand that sex is a taboo topic, something secret that you shouldn't talk about, and probably wrong—something special, secret, and bad. And since the parents won't talk about it, the child isn't very likely to bring up the subject by asking questions.

I've heard parents argue that their daughter is young and innocent and needs protection from all the ugly things they read about in the papers. They simply don't realize that children can't be protected by keeping them ignorant, even if that were possible. If they don't get information at home, they'll get it somewhere else, and chances are it won't be correct. Every sex therapist knows that ignorance is at the root of much sex-connected misery.

Speaking now to teen-age girls, let me say that I understand you probably have your own difficulties talking about sex with your parents, but you're learning about it every day just the same, in school and elsewhere. For instance, your feelings about a teacher may be telling you something. Even more likely, your feelings about a particular boy may not seem sexual at the time but quite possibly can be a cover-up for a beginning sexual interest in him.

One of the easiest ways of getting to talk about sex with your parents is through discussing stories in the newspapers. Sex is often news these days; the papers are filled with it. You may read these stories without really understanding them, and if you're not afraid to ask questions, you can ask about such things as contraception, abortion, adultery, illegitimacy, child molesting, rape, and other matters. If your parents have enough knowledge themselves to give you the right answers, you can put into perspective things that might otherwise be frightening or mystifying to you. Such things as attempted censorship of books, movies, or rock lyrics also provide openings. Even a story about how good nutrition relates to early puberty can be an opportunity for discussion.

I hope parents reading these words understand that giving a child information is one thing and lecturing them is another, as Madonna advised in her hit single, "Papa, Don't Preach." Nothing turns off a child faster, especially teen-agers. Talking about sex should be a calm, objective exchange of feelings and information and views, without making a point of it.

Some parents have a false fear that if they bring up sexual topics themselves, it will stimulate a child's interest in sex, and that talking about it will lead to experimenting. They don't understand that interest and experimentation have probably been going on for some time. Besides, children who are both curious and ignorant about sex will try to find out anyway. They're going to explore their own bodies, and probably those of their playmates as well. That idea may frighten some parents, but there's no need to worry. No harm is done by preadolescent sex play, which nearly all children do in one way or another.

So the question isn't *what* girls do sexually but how they feel about what they're doing, and what kinds of relationships they develop with other people. These are the factors that help determine what kind of human beings they turn out to be.

A few differences between boys and girls affect their attitudes and sexual behavior with each other. One of the most striking differences is that boys are more oriented toward their genitals, generally speaking, and are a little more concerned with genital activity. A girl is more interested in the things surrounding sex than with sex itself. If girls and boys understood this simple fact, they'd be better able to get along with each other.

Another difference is the greater concern the girl has for her reputation, not only where her peers are concerned but in the adult world. This traditional difference, however, seems to be changing, too, and may even be vanishing rather rapidly. Parents have done the most to create this difference and keep it alive, not realizing that girls may determine what they do or don't do sexually mostly on the basis of what other people may think about them, rather than on what their true feelings may be. In the new climate that girls and women inhabit today, however, even these standards are disappearing. There aren't many families remaining in which girls are still taught to be "lady-like," meaning feminine, demure, nonaggressive, with dresses down and legs crossed, and are told not to "chase the boys." Those ideas are relics of grand-mother's day.

Girls understand now that they are far more likely to make good social and sexual adjustments to life if they learn to be warm, open, responsive, and sexually unafraid. They've learned to be sexual *partners* of men, with equal needs, responses, and responsibilities—no longer simply possessions. With some men, of course, it's still a male world with the females subordinate, but the walls are crumbling.

Some girls are lucky enough to learn all this from their mothers as role models; some are not. Those mothers who are openly affectionate, warm, and lov-ing toward their daughters and their husbands are more likely to have happy and well-adjusted girls in their families. It's right to be as open, relaxed, and objective about sex as it's possible to be. Parents who find that hard to do need to review their own sex lives and ask themselves whether they've been so free of guilt and fear that they've never had any problems.

Knowledge, let me say once more, is the most im-portant element. In the pages that follow, I've tried to supply the latest and most reliable information about the sex lives of girls in a way they'll understand, one that will help them fulfill their roles in this complicated world.

CHAPTER · 1

Growing Up in a New Sexual World

If you're a girl growing up today, you may think you know everything there is to know about sex. Unlike your mother and grandmother, you see sex on the movie screen and television, hear about it in rock lyrics, read about it in newspapers, magazines, and books. We're supersaturated with sex, and there's nothing new. But if that's so, why is it that the offices of sex therapists everywhere in the country are filled with people who are having all kinds of problems—many of them the same old problems—and why is it that most of these problems are the result of ignorance? Could it be that people think they know more about sex than they do? The answer is yes, especially in the case of preadolescents and many adolescents, who don't really understand what they're seeing and hearing.

If you're curious and looking for information, you want it to be accurate, in the first place, and not preachy or moralistic. That's why I wrote this book and the one that accompanies it, *Boys and Sex.* Over the past twenty years, these books have been read all over the world, and experience shows that both sexes have read and profited from each other's books.

I had another reason for writing, however. I wanted to show what results might be expected from different kinds of sexual behavior, and to talk about the meaning such behavior could have for different individuals. "Meaning" isn't the same for everyone, of course. Sex means different things to different people. For some, the word means simply reproduction. To others, it means behavior, like the changes in the body that occur when someone is sexually aroused. Changes can result from various kinds of psychological stimulation, or they can be caused by self-stimulation or by another person.

Some people have a much broader idea of sex. To them it means how a girl acts and feels simply because she's a girl trying to find out what role she's to play in our society. A library of books could be compiled in which each one would look at sex in different ways. I'll have a few things to say about that in this book, but mostly I'm going to talk about sex as a specific kind of behavior, and about what meaning it might have for a preteen or teen-age girl.

I expect more parents will be upset, more than they

were with *Boys and Sex,* because they think girls aren't ready for such information at an early age, but as I pointed out in the Introduction, this is a dangerous kind of parental blindness. The fact is that both boys and girls, if they're going to have sexual relations with each other, or even think they might have them, need an equal amount of information. In the past girls were put at a disadvantage with the excuse of "protecting" them. Now they're entitled to the same information.

Before you begin reading, you may want to know what *my* attitudes are about sex. First, I believe we need *understanding* by both girls and boys about sex more than anything else. That's the only way they can ever find happiness and fulfillment in each other. The key is that overworked but useful word *communication.* Most of us need to learn how to communicate with one another. That means simply being honest and open, not afraid to let the other person know how we feel, especially in sexual matters. Sex itself is one of the most important ways people communicate. Sometimes it can be a great experience, but it can also be a bad one if it's hostile or hurtful.

That's why I say that both boys and girls think they know more about sex than they do. It's a subject more complex than most people realize, even those who take it for granted and believe the whole thing is simple. If it were that simple, it wouldn't have been written about and discussed for centuries at such extraordinary length.

We know sex is important in everyone's life, but even professionals are not entirely agreed about what its role is in the life of preteens and teens. Some say sexual intercourse is only for adults, and they don't think young teen-agers are able to handle it. They advocate setting reasonable limits, meaning that girls and boys should feel free to experiment sexually, which they'll do anyway, but that they shouldn't go beyond fondling each other to orgasm. Others advocate more freedom, some less.

I think everyone can agree, however, that teen-age sex should be a learning experience, not a frightening one. Setting certain limits may make it less likely to be frightening, especially for very young girls. Of course, the question of whether a girl should engage in *any* kind of sexual behavior depends on the attitude of the people with whom she lives, especially those of her own age. Other factors are the social level on which she lives; the problems of inner-city children and those in the suburbs and rural areas aren't always the same, as well as the system of values, ethics, codes, or religion a girl has chosen to guide her. In any case, I believe that whatever a girl decides to do about sex should be based on as much information as possible, and that's the kind I want to provide here.

I have a few other convictions about sex. In the past, I think, we've put far too much emphasis on the question of intercourse before marriage. In the new climate of acceptance we live in, it's clear that what's important in the relationship between two people is how they feel about each other, not whether a penis enters a vagina.

My basic feeling is that sexual behavior for both

boys and girls is something that's pleasurable and desirable, just as long as certain rules are followed:

1. Don't do anything to hurt someone else, or go against the other person's wishes or desires. In short, be responsible toward the other person.
2. Whatever you do, do it so that the other person doesn't get into trouble.
3. Respect those who choose not to engage in any sexual experiences. That's their right.

Now that you know *my* attitudes, I'm sure you've already begun to agree or disagree. What I hope is that you'll also begin to examine more closely what your *own* attitudes are about sex, and why you feel the way you do—or why you may not know exactly *how* you feel.

If you're confused about sex, the first thing is to find a path out of the confusion, one that's yours alone. Begin by thinking for a minute about the real differences between boys and girls. Not the obvious differences in anatomy, but the way the two sexes approach life, the roles they play in society, and their sexual lives. As a member of the present generation, you're in a much better position to do that kind of analyzing than any before you, because you're living at a time when the role of women is undergoing a major change, with resulting confusion in which many of the traditional differences between the sexes are now disappearing, as I observed earlier. Now that we understand girls have sexual needs much the same as boys, the old double standard that has prevailed for centuries is disappearing at last. But even when all the changes are recognized, there are differences that remain, and it's important to understand them. Both teen-agers and adults have trouble really understanding sex, but in the increasingly complex society we live in today, it's necessary to make the attempt at understanding because sex problems are a factor in a great many divorces, even in cases where they're not the chief factor. For those who stay married, the situation isn't much different. There are still enough sex problems to keep doctors, sex therapists, clergymen, marriage counselors, and other kinds of therapists busy.

What are these *real* differences between the sexes? For boys, sex is often an awareness of changes in their bodies—physical changes that happen when they're sexually aroused. That can happen when they see pictures, read books, hear stories, think of sexy situations, touch people of the opposite sex or the same sex, or touch their own bodies. Arousal means that the blood rushes to the surface of the skin and makes it warm; the penis hardens and becomes erect, increasing in size from about three-and-a-half to six inches; and the breath comes faster. These things can happen every day of their lives.

Girls often don't know that this is happening to boys, and don't realize it can even be a source of embarrassment to them, especially when they have to stand up in class and discover they have an erection. Boys are afraid others will see the bulge in their jeans.

When a boy goes out with a girl, his awkwardness and shyness may mean he's fighting against the sexual response he feels. Even if the girl is completely unaware of it, the boy doesn't know that. All he knows is how embarrassed he'd be if she knew.

When girls are aroused, they go through the same kind of bodily changes boys do—that is, they feel warm and flushed and their breath comes faster. Instead of an erection, their genital area becomes damp because arousal has activated glands that lubricate the vagina, so that in intercourse, if it occurred, the penis would slip in more easily. Girls who have never been aroused to that point are usually surprised if they find out other girls have had such sensations.

If this kind of stimulation continues, in both boys and girls, it will increase in intensity until a pitch of excitement is reached that may be uncontrollable. At that point, sometimes a sudden release of sexual tension occurs, a kind of explosion that varies in intensity, followed by a quiet, relaxed, blissful feeling. This release of tension is what we call an "orgasm," or sexual climax. Sometimes it happens when people fondle each other, or it may happen (and most often does) during intercourse, or when a girl or boy rubs the sex organ. It can even happen at night while a boy (or girl) is dreaming about sex. That's called a "nocturnal emission."

Some girls understand why their response to sexual stimulation isn't the same as it is for boys, even though the reaction may be much the same physically. They can see why it is that boys feel more at home with sex. It's because sex is so much a part of their lives. Girls have sexual needs and desires, too, and respond when they're aroused, but most, particularly the younger ones, are still restrained about expressing their feelings, even though they have a freedom they never had before. Tradition dies hard, and many parents, perhaps most, still exert pressure on their daughters to follow rules, at least for as long as they can maintain any kind of authority role. Such restrictions usually irritate girls, who naturally don't like being grounded when they break the rules.

But no matter what the relationship between daughter and parents may be, in the end it's the girl who decides when she feels mature enough to handle sexual situations with boys. Some parents may still believe that a girl suddenly becomes a sexual being when she gets married, but very few girls have that illusion. Today they may not want to marry at all, or they may want to delay marriage until their careers are well launched. Meanwhile, they expect to experience their own sexuality—at their own time and their own pace.

For boys, arousal and erection begin a drive toward orgasm, if they have the opportunity. Studies of sexual behavior show this in a dramatic way. By the time they're fifteen, nearly all boys are having orgasm on the average of two or three times a week. For two-thirds of them, their first orgasm comes from masturbation; for one-fifth, from sexual dreams; and for less than one-sixth, from fondling a girl. Less than one in ten has had orgasm from intercourse. Most boys keep on having orgasm from masturbation.

It's a different story with girls. Only about half the girls have been aroused at all by any means at fifteen, according to the Kinsey Report of more than thirty years ago, but certainly that figure would be higher today. Even in that earlier study, however, it was clear that rapid changes took place in the next five years. At the age of twenty, about nine out of ten had experienced some kind of arousal. At fifteen only a fourth had an orgasm from any source, but five years later the figure was more than half. About a third were aroused by masturbation, a third by being fondled, and another third through psychological stimulation—books, fantasies, dreams, or whatever. Two-fifths experienced their first orgasm from masturbation, one in twenty from dreams, a fourth from being fondled, one in ten from premarital intercourse, a surprising one in six from marital intercourse, and 3 percent from homosexual contacts. All these figures, as I've said, are undoubtedly higher today, perhaps much higher, but unfortunately we have no comprehensive studies to confirm this.

Statistics are often dull, but here are a few that will tell you something about why you may be having trouble with your boyfriend. Nearly all boys have orgasms at fifteen, and they have them two or three times a week. They're going out with girls of the same age, more or less, but three-fourths of *them* aren't having any orgasms at all. The other fourth have one only once every two weeks. No wonder there's trouble when two adolescents with such widely different sex experiences go out together. It's easy to see why so much misunderstanding occurs.

The problem is that males are sexually mature and active at thirteen or earlier, but girls develop more slowly sexually, in spite of the fact that biologically they're ready for sex at increasingly earlier times. A boy is at his sexual peak during adolescence, and then becomes gradually less active as he grows older, although some men are still active in their nineties. Women develop more gradually. They reach a peak of responsiveness in their thirties, forties, or even fifties. Their response is not only as great as the men's but can be even more intense. Consequently the problems of adolescence can go right on into adult life, and they're not easily solved unless there's real understanding on both sides.

Important sexual differences exist among girls themselves, and people often find it hard to understand that there's a wide range of sexual interest and responsiveness among them. By "people," I mean boys especially. They usually have no idea that there are some girls who are simply not interested in sex at that point in their lives. They also don't understand that many girls are not easily aroused by pictures, books, or by what they see in the movies, unlike boys. But that doesn't mean they're apathetic about boys. They may like them, and want to go out with them and enjoy their company. Sex simply hasn't yet become a part of their conscious lives.

Not all girls are in this category, of course. A relatively small number are even more easily aroused than boys by seeing, reading, and thinking of sexual things. They have orgasms frequently, quickly, and easily, and have a real struggle to keep out of trouble in a society that may try to restrict their behavior. They may also have difficulty in their own teen-age society if most of the other girls aren't as uninhibited, which is usually the case.

Between these two extremes is a large class of girls, of whom most are much closer to the "unresponsive" end of the scale than to the uninhibited end.

With such differences among themselves, and between themselves and boys, girls often find it hard to adjust to the world they live in. Even with the new freedom and acceptance, the community they inhabit still has its rules and its expectations of their general behavior. Yet everything they see and hear encourages them to break the rules. They resent that girls in general are all lumped together, regardless of their differences.

For example, if a girl has sex with a boy, she steps out of the role society has assigned to her at that age, and often both she and the boy wind up being confused about what's happened to them. Or a girl may reject what her parents and society think, but then she has to be aware that there may be penalties to pay if what she's doing becomes known. It's easy for a girl to be confused if she sees permissiveness all around her while she's subjected to the social pressures put on her by parents and other members of the adult community. Sometimes these girls don't know where to turn or how to behave.

In that case, it may be fortunate that sex isn't as much of a problem for girls as it is for boys, by and large, nor even as much of a problem as their parents may think it is. Sex, in fact, is less important to girls than their public image. By contrast, boys aren't as concerned about their sexual reputations and may even be proud to be considered "studs." Girls, however, are often painfully conscious of what other people think of them, and especially what other girls think. In spite of their new freedom, they're still fearful of getting a bad reputation, or of being known as easy marks for boys who want sex, or of being outside the accepted social pattern.

Girls don't talk about sex, as sex, the way boys do, generally speaking. Boys talk about sex a lot. They constantly trade information or make jokes about it. Much of what they think they know may be wrong, and they're inclined to exaggerate their own sexual exploits.

On the other hand, girls' conversation centers on going out, and clothes, and the personalities of individual boys, not on their probable availability for sex or on specific sexual activities. Their view of sex is more romantic, and that's something boys ought to know and remember.

If a girl is asked, "Do you have any sex dreams at night?" she'll often answer, "Yes," and if she's asked about the content of her dreams, what she tells you shows quite clearly the difference between what boys and girls mean when they say "sex." The girl will say she dreamed about being with a boy somewhere, having fun with him that isn't necessarily sexual. If she says she dreamed of making love with a boy, it usually turns out that she didn't mean intercourse, or even mutual fondling, but something dreamlike, warm, and affectionate happening between her and a boy she likes.

This kind of romantic feeling is what girls usually dream about, awake or asleep, rather than some particular kind of sexual behavior. Her night dreams and daytime fantasies are quite different from what boys experience. Boys dream or fantasize about fondling a girl in different ways, including all the details, possibly including intercourse, and experiencing one sexual sensation after another.

Girls are rarely so specific. For them, the dream or the fantasy is a romantic setting in which they experience a warm and happy feeling of being with a boy.

As I said earlier, it's too bad that girls can't talk with their parents about sex. They might understand themselves better. But it's no more possible for them in most cases than it is for the boys. Fathers find it especially difficult to talk with daughters because so many of them don't want to think about their being involved sexually with boys. They have a legitimate fear that a daughter might get pregnant, but a large part of their problem is the reluctance to admit that their little girls are growing up. Normally, fathers are jealous of this maturing. They don't want to give up their daughters to boys, who are seen subconsciously as male rivals.

As for mothers, they've lived through this adolescent period themselves and have struggled with the same problems. Most of them have known what it is to worry about when to have some kind of sexual activity with boys, to be curious about sex and look for answers no one appears to want to give. Whatever their adolescent experience happened to be, they're likely to transfer it to their daughters.

I'm sure that what I've told you here isn't going to solve the daughter-parent problem for most girls, but it may help you to understand better what may have seemed like unreasonable demands from your parents.

What else should a girl know about sex as she grows up, and after she understands the fundamental differences between herself and boys?

I think she ought to know something about the sexual parts of her own body, to become familiar and comfortable with it. She should have the same knowledge about boys. She ought to know what causes the changes in her body when she's sexually aroused. She ought to have some insight into her early sexual experiences and understand what effect they may have on her later life. It would also be helpful to have more information about her *social* relations with boys—going out with them, for example—and about sexual relations, too—specifically, sexual activity that stops short of intercourse.

A girl also ought to know what intercourse is like

and understand what's involved, pro and con, before she commits herself to it. In short, how she can tell when she's emotionally ready for sex. Few girls these days wait until they're married. For a long time now, therapists and feminist writers have been stressing how important it is for a girl to know something about the stimulation of her own body and to have a better understanding of the meaning of sexual relations between members of the same sex. She needs to know how different boys and girls can be when it comes to sexual behavior and attitudes, in ways I've already touched on. All this will determine to a major extent how good her sexual adjustment will be, either in marriage or in some other relationship.

If a girl has such a body of knowledge, I think she'll come to understand that she will have to be something of an actress in life. Clearly she's been given three roles to play. One is her role in society, first as a young girl growing up, then as a wife and mother, or as a career girl, or a combination of both. A second role is her relationship with boys as she grows up, in which she has to learn to adjust to social roles and at the same time develop her own sexuality. It's the third role that's most difficult—the role she must play as herself, an individual responsible to herself.

No actress in the theater or the movies could have a more difficult combination of roles. As an adolescent, she's engaged in learning how to adjust to society, to the adult world. Yet she has to get along with boys, who may have the same expectations of her as the adult world does, and at the same time regard her as a sexual object, no matter how much feminists may protest the fact. Yet in spite of all this, a girl has her own self, her own feelings, to consider. It isn't easy.

My hope is that the information in the following chapters will truly help girls to play their triple role in a way that will bring them into the adult world with the best prospects for a reasonably happy life.

CHAPTER · 2

Learning About Your Body

"What a funny way to put it," you may be thinking—
"learning about my *body*? What is there to know? I can
see it, and feel it for myself." But oddly enough,
preteens often don't understand the commonplace
things that are happening to them as they grow up,
and some carry this lack of knowledge right into adolescence. Maybe you believe you're just as happy not
knowing, but knowing is more comfortable.

All this is particularly true for girls, who have more
to think about where their bodies are concerned than
boys do. In some ways, of course, they develop the
same as boys as they approach puberty and pass
through it into adolescence. Both experience changes

in body size and shape, in the breasts and sex organs. For girls, the most important change is when menstruation begins, because after that, it's possible for them to conceive and bear children.

Real change begins usually about the time a girl is twelve years old, although it can happen earlier or later; there's no rule about it. In fact, the average age has been dropping slowly over the past few decades; girls seem to be maturing earlier. Some girls have pubic hair and developing breasts when they're as young as eight or nine, while others don't exhibit those signs until they're fifteen or older. We don't know all the reasons for these wide variations, but one of them is certainly what a girl inherits from her parents, making her predisposed to develop early or late. Nutrition is another factor. Girls with better nutrition develop earlier, while those who don't eat properly as they grow up tend to develop later.

While it makes no difference in a sexual sense whether a girl develops early or late, it *does* matter to her socially. Every girl (and every boy, too) gets a sense of well-being from the knowledge that she is like the people around her. Consequently the early and late developers feel that they're different from their friends—very tall or very short girls, for instance—and they may be uncomfortable about it. Such differences may affect a girl's social outlook, but if we're talking only about sexual development, she can find some consolation in the fact that, either way, the others will be more or less like her eventually, or she'll be like them. Of course, some girls are naturally tall and some naturally short, but that's usually a matter of heredity, and nothing can be done about it.

Probably the part of body development that most worries girls is their breasts. It's unfair, but our society has put a premium on ample breasts, and girls think they won't be attractive to boys if they don't have fairly large breasts—an idea feminists haven't been able to eliminate from what teen-agers think about themselves. Adolescent girls go through a great deal of unnecessary worry about their breasts, mostly because they believe what Nature gave them is too small. There's much less worry over whether they're too large, and a few worry (even more unnecessarily) because they get the idea that their breasts are developing unevenly.

The fact is that breasts, like every other part of the anatomy, come in all sizes, and appear to be attached to the body in a variety of ways. While it's possible for plastic surgeons to increase or decrease the size of breasts, it isn't something that ought to be done only because a girl, or a woman, thinks she may be more attractive. As they grow up, most girls realize that size isn't important to anyone but themselves. The emphasis on breasts in our culture—through advertising, the movies, magazines, and television—has done considerable damage to innumerable girls. It isn't new, of course. Stylish emphasis on breasts has existed in other centuries and other cultures, but the power of the media today makes more of an impression. The emphasis on large breasts has made millions of girls with small breasts feel inferior and has given them the false idea that they'll be less attractive as sexual partners.

Girls should remember that few of them (or adult women, for that matter) are built like movie and television stars, yet there doesn't seem to be any difficulty in finding sexual partners, other things being equal. Even before the women's movement pointed it out, many girls knew that there were far more important things that made them attractive to boys they liked. What they didn't know, and most still do not, is that breasts become larger temporarily during sexual arousal, sometimes by as much as 25 percent. In any case, you can be sure that boys are going to like you for yourself, not for your cup size.

Unfortunately, girls who spend a lot of time worrying about their breasts often don't know and understand the rest of their anatomy. It's amazing but true that girls rarely examine their own sex organs to see how they're put together. It's a little more difficult for them than it is for boys, whose organs are visible and accessible. It's universally true of males that they examine their own penises and scrotums. If girls had a little more curiosity, it would repay them to hold a mirror in one hand and part their pubic hair with the other. If they did, they would understand their own anatomy considerably better.

What they would see first is a primary difference between the sexes. Girls have one more body opening than boys. Both have the anus, from which the body's solid waste materials are excreted, but there the resemblance ends. The boy has another opening, at the end of his penis, out of which he discharges urine and the sperm-laden fluid of his ejaculation. But the girl has a special opening to discharge the urine and a third opening between the urinary outlet (the urethra) and the anus. It's called the vagina. She also has, near the top of the vulva (the collective term we use for all the sex organs visible outside the body) a tiny organ called the clitoris. It's a small organ with a rich supply of nerve endings, and when it's stimulated, it provides sexual pleasure. The vulva also includes two folds of skin—an outer one, called the labia majora, and an inner one, the labia minora.

The vagina is simply a passageway between the external vulva and the internal sex organs, which include the uterus or womb, the ovaries, and the Fallopian tubes. All of these are encased within the protective framework of the pelvis, that part of the abdominal cavity lying between the hipbones.

A vagina is a remarkable organ, no matter how it's viewed. Its walls have an astonishing flexibility, so that no matter how large a penis may be, it can hardly test the capacity of an organ whose walls are able to stretch and stretch enough to permit a baby to be born. That's truly remarkable, if you know that the vagina, on the average, is only three to three-and-a-half inches long. It's an organ with many uses. It provides a canal for the menstrual flow; it receives the penis in intercourse; it holds the sperm cells when the male has discharged them and starts them on their journey upward. Finally it provides the pathway for a baby's birth.

In all these functions, the vagina gets some help

from its own lubrication system. Fluid comes from glands in the cervix, to which the vagina is attached at the upper end, and is lubricated still further by other glands near the outer opening. Mostly, however, it's lubricated by internal secretions from its own walls when they get warm in response to sexual stimulation —much like sweat on the body. A girl feels these secretions. She becomes wet around the vulva and possibly on her thighs when she's sexually aroused.

Over the entrance to the vagina is a thin membrane called the hymen, with an opening in it that allows menstrual fluid to pass through. The hymen is flexible enough so that a tampon can be inserted, usually without breaking it. Girls used to worry that when they had their first intercourse and the hymen was broken, the result would be pain and blood. But the pain is usually no more than a brief twinge, and the blood only a trickle if it occurs at all. In any event, hymens are often broken these days long before first intercourse takes place. This has been true for some time now, ever since women began to participate actively in sports and to go on exercise regimes. Hymens are also broken sometimes when girls masturbate by putting a finger or some other object into the vagina. Often the hymen breaks so easily a girl doesn't even know when it happens. Only rarely is it so tough that a doctor will be needed to break it.

Girls who have been blissfully unconscious of their sex organs while they're very young suddenly become very much aware of them when they begin to menstruate. That usually occurs about a year after the appearance of pubic hair and the beginning of breast development. But again, there's considerable variation among girls, and it may not happen at exactly that time. There's no reason to worry if it doesn't happen until later. Like other symptoms of sexual development, it doesn't matter whether it's early or late.

If some girls react badly to adolescent changes in their bodies, it's because they sense that life has now become different from what it's been for so long. Some girls simply don't like the idea of growing up. And anyway, for everybody, menstruation seems like a messy business. If they happen to have cramps, or other aches and pains, as some girls and women do, they resent this intrusion into their lives every month. When they realize it's something that's going to happen to them for the next twenty-five to forty years, a few girls even feel trapped and are seized with a kind of despair.

Most girls, however, take it all in stride. They're even pleased by the onset of menstruation because they *do* want to grow up, and they understand that this is one of the most important parts of that process. Menstruation means becoming a woman.

It helps to have an understanding parent when menstruation begins. I knew a father who observed the occasion of his daughter's first menstruation by bringing her flowers and making a little ceremony of the fact that now she had become a young woman. A good many girls today would find that embarrassing, I suppose, but anything a parent can do to make a daughter feel proud and good about becoming an adolescent is helpful.

When we've said all this, however, it's still true that for many girls menstruation comes as a dismaying shock. This is especially true when there's been so little communication between parents and children about sex that a girl is completely unprepared for it. Not every girl gets what we used to call "the facts of life" from other sources. When menstruation does begin, most mothers tell their daughters what to do about it, and that's also when the girls often learn that it will be with them for most of their lives. Unfortunately, mothers don't usually provide any more than the most basic information.

Yet there isn't anything mysterious about it. What's happened is that inside the girl's body her ovaries have begun to function. These organs, one on each side of the uterus, carry the eggs that create another life when they're combined with a male sperm. One of these eggs matures every month (usually), and about halfway between periods of menstruation, it breaks loose from the follicle that encloses it in the ovary and moves down into the Fallopian tube. The follicle is only a covering for the egg, but it also has the function of producing the female sex hormone, estrogen, which provides a girl with the characteristics identifying her as female. Its companion ovarian hormone, progesterone, prepares the uterine lining for pregnancy, if the egg is fertilized by the sperm.

After the egg has left it, the follicle changes color and becomes something else, called "the yellow body." It's larger now, and it begins to affect the lining of the uterus, providing it with blood pools concentrated under the cell layers so that the baby will have oxygen and food if conception occurs.

If fertilization *doesn't* take place, however, the whole scene changes. The egg simply disintegrates in a few hours and disappears. The yellow body goes too, since it no longer has any purpose. What remains are the blood pools it created, but since the body isn't equipped to take these back into the circulatory system, the blood and the cell layers in the lining of the uterus slip out through the vagina. And that's what we call menstruation.

Girls who fear they're passing too much blood should know that they're losing only about one to three ounces of it. Menstrual blood isn't like the blood that spurts out when you cut yourself, because it's mixed with the mucous membrane from the womb. A girl shouldn't feel squeamish about it, although some do. People frequently have intercourse during menstruation and feel entirely comfortable.

There's no reason to worry if menstruation is irregular when it first begins. Sometimes several months elapse between the first and second times, and it's perfectly natural for young girls to be irregular. It only means that the ovaries haven't yet begun to produce mature eggs on a regular basis. Nor is there any reason to worry about the length of the period. Sometimes it takes only three days, sometimes as much as seven. Five days is the average, but a girl might not always menstruate for the same number of days every time.

Some girls have their period regularly, have no forewarning until it begins, and experience no symptoms of any kind, except maybe a feeling of fullness. Some have only the common symptom, cramps. But others also feel depressed and vaguely unhappy; their bodies seem heavy and lumpy, and they're listless and tired for a day or two. This feeling can be produced by a combination of psychological and physical factors. The best remedies are aspirin and a little mild exercise. If there's any danger, it's that a girl will take her symptoms so seriously that she will use menstruation as an excuse to retreat from life into illness every month in order to get attention or to avoid some situation in her life.

There's no reason for a girl to feel crippled or out of the running when she's menstruating. If she does, she should see her doctor. Normally she can do nearly everything she's accustomed to doing, except it's probably a good idea not to exercise too violently on the first day. It's only a superstition that a girl can't take a bath or a shower or go in swimming or wash her hair when she's menstruating. She only needs to be a little careful about getting chilled, because her body is more susceptible to chilling at that particular time. A healthy girl can exercise, go to classes, work, go to parties, or do anything else she likes while she's menstruating. She'll feel better if she gets enough sleep, and if she takes in more fluids than usual—fruit juice and milk, for example—and if she avoids rich, starchy food. But that's good advice for anybody.

Some girls are bothered and feel self-conscious about the odor of menstruation and the increased activity of the sweat glands that accompanies it. Personal hygiene is an easy answer to that problem. Use deodorants under the arms. Tampons or sanitary pads should be changed frequently.

Some girls like pads, others prefer tampons, which seem to be the most popular today. Many use pads the first day or two, then switch to tampons. It's a personal choice. I believe there may be a good psychological reason for using tampons, because they teach a girl what it's like to have something in her vagina, and maybe that will make her more comfortable when she has intercourse. Sometimes a girl needs to be taught how to insert them properly. They should never be forced in. It's often helpful to lubricate the tip of the tampon before insertion. Even with minimal flow, they should be changed every four hours. Incidentally, there's no proof that using tampons will cause cancer.

Menstruation isn't the only kind of discharge to come from the vagina. There may be, sometimes, a slight bloody staining between periods, but it's nothing to worry about. It may happen as the egg leaves the ovary and moves down into the uterus. A girl may even feel a little brief pain on one side or the other. However, that isn't true of all girls, or women, and those who experience it may have it for as little as a half hour or as long as a day. But if there's genuine bleeding between periods—that is, much thicker and darker than the staining—or if the periods are very difficult, a girl should consult her doctor at once. Such bleeding isn't normal, and the difficulty may require medical attention.

Another kind of vaginal discharge can occur. It's a seepage of fluid ranging from white to yellow in color, often with a noticeable odor plus some itching or burning. That's sometimes caused by a fungus growth resulting from germs that have found their way into the vagina. A doctor can cure it easily with medication. If this problem occurs, girls shouldn't feel so embarrassed that they won't even tell their mothers. If they don't do anything, the infection may continue for some time. But it's no more special than a minor infection anywhere else in the body. Tell your mother and get it taken care of promptly by a doctor.

All the above is what you need to know about menstruation. Now let's look at what happens when the vagina is penetrated by a male penis in intercourse and pregnancy results. It's surprising that even in this era of sexual freedom and plenty of information there are a good many girls who don't really understand this process.

It isn't such a simple cause-and-effect relationship as it may seem. When the male ejaculates, he pours his semen into the vagina. It contains million of sperm cells whose long tails begin to lash, moving them forward until they enter the cervix, the passageway into the uterus, or womb. The uterus is pear-shaped. It looks a little like the head of a very small bull, with the Fallopian tubes as its horns, connecting the uterus with the ovaries. The sperm swim from the cervix into the uterus and up through these "horns." There they may or may not encounter an unfertilized egg cell coming down from the ovary on the once-a-month descent through the tubes.

If the sperm encounter an egg in the tubes, a bombardment of it results as the tiny sperm cells, lashing their tails, surround it and try to penetrate it. Pregnancy occurs when a sperm cell enters through the egg wall and merges with the egg, after which the cell wall immediately hardens up so that no more sperm can get in. The sperm cell that did the fertilizing becomes a part of the egg's nucleus. The other sperm die in a few hours. This whole process, from ejaculation to the encounter with the egg cell, may take as long as eight hours.

When sperm and egg join, fertilization takes place and the baby is conceived at that moment. (Whether life begins then, in a medical sense, is a matter of scientific dispute.) Sperm carrying Y chromosomes make boys; those with X chromosomes make girls. Sex is determined by whatever kind of sperm cell fertilizes the egg cell, and that's a matter of pure chance. In fact, chance plays a large part in the whole process. The sperm must be in the Fallopian tubes at a time when the egg is traveling through them. In addition, it must be a vigorous sperm and the egg must be ripe. A woman produces only about 400 ripe eggs in her entire lifetime, and there are only about twelve to twenty-four hours in every month when it's possible for a ripe egg to be fertilized.

If these odds against pregnancy encourage a girl and boy to "take a chance," they should remember that sexual Russian roulette is a dangerous game, and in the end the odds are against them. The risk is far too great.

Just as there are many misconceptions about getting pregnant, there are probably nearly as many about childbirth. Sometimes girls hear so many horror stories about the agony of birth and the distress of pregnancy itself that they're badly frightened of getting pregnant even if they're married, and if they do, they live in a state of fear until the baby comes. Fortunately those feelings are being rapidly outdated. Most girls now know about "natural" childbirth, and for those at the other end of the opinion scale, modern drugs can alleviate much of the pain. Women have a variety of choices today, and the old fears seem to be disappearing. In natural childbirth, for example, women are taught how to give birth without the aid of anesthetics, learning to take part in the process in an active way so that they participate in the experience. Men are often drawn into the birth process, too, as husbands go into the delivery room and share with their wives what's happening, making it more meaningful for both of them.

As I said earlier, girls who wonder how anything as large as a baby can come out of anything as relatively small as a vagina simply underestimate the incredible stretching capacity of that organ. It's the stretching of the cervix that causes pain, but many women have learned to have little fear of it by absorbing the techniques of natural childbirth.

For those who can't accept these techniques, modern anesthetics can help to decrease the pain. In any case there's little danger in properly supervised childbirth these days. For one thing, women see their doctor regularly during pregnancy, and the physician is consequently able to anticipate any possible complications. True, complications *can* occur, but the chances are extremely low. For those that can occur during the last three months, the odds are about one in two hundred that they'll ever happen, and even then, if doctor and patient work together, any trouble can either be prevented or taken care of as soon as it happens.

As for the discomfort involved during pregnancy or birth, millions of women will testify that it's more than made up for, many times over, by the special joy of giving birth to a baby.

What you have just read in this chapter covers the cycle of change in a girl from the time of her beginning adolescence until she has her first child. Some of my readers are probably in the first part of that cycle, and I hope they've found here the information they need to understand how their bodies are constructed and will be encouraged to investigate and appreciate how marvelously equipped they are to function as one half of the male-female relationship.

For the older girls the culmination of their physical

development usually comes at about the time they reach sixteen. A girl who's arrived at that age and still hasn't reached physical maturity should remember that the widest possible variation exists in the human female, as well as the male. Look around and you'll see girls who are only ten or eleven, yet they've reached their full development in growth and height. Look again and you'll see others who are sixteen and still haven't reached it and may not until they're twenty-one or even older in a few cases. Even when growth and height are complete, there's still further development in the breasts and the growth of pubic hair. In fact, a girl's figure may keep on filling out for some time, until it's reached the proportions she'll have as a woman.

As I'm sure you already know, adolescence can be a joyous and happy time, but also a period of change and adjustment, which is often painful. For some it means anxiety and fear. The girl who has a good knowledge of her body will find it much easier to enjoy the process of growing up—and every girl has to go through it.

CHAPTER · 3

Discovering Sex

If you think back to your earliest memories, chances are that one of them will have something to do with sex and your discovery of it. It's natural for both boys and girls to be curious about what the sex organs of the opposite sex look like, and they find ways to satisfy their curiosity. By the time they're five years old, about six out of ten girls have seen a male's penis. Often it's a younger brother who offers the first sight while he's being bathed or diapered as his sister watches.

But even if a girl has a baby brother, one out of every ten girls hasn't seen the penis of a living male by the time she's thirteen. Parents often keep a girl from viewing it, and of course that only stimulates her interest in seeing something that's forbidden. In the worst case, it may make her fearful and ashamed to look at a penis, and that will be a sure source of trouble later on.

Whatever parents may think they're doing by hiding the penis, it won't have the good end results they imagine it will. Instead there may be psychological damage, and it will be a wholly unnecessary risk in any event because girls who read magazines or illustrated art books are bound to see the penis reproduced in works of painting and sculpture. Great masters have reproduced it endlessly through the ages—Michelangelo's magnificent "David" is a superb example—just as they have reproduced both the male and the female nude body in all its splendor. Museums are filled with their testimonials to the beauty of the human form. It doesn't happen nearly as often anymore, but if a girl gets the idea when she's very young that the penis (and the nude male body) is ugly or repulsive, she'll have a lot to overcome when she gets to the point of having sexual relationships with men.

It's far better for her to see her little brother's penis, or that of some other boy, in the casual pattern of everyday living, and so learn to accept it as a simple fact of life. If it's hidden, she'll keep on wondering about it, and such secrecy can mean nothing but trouble later on.

About half of all girls have seen their father's penis, or that of an older male relative, by the time they become adolescent. The experience means little more to them than seeing a baby's or a small boy's penis. They're just things males have, and their curiosity is at least partly satisfied. But merely seeing the male sex organ and actually having sexual contact with adult males are two quite different things. I'll discuss that problem later on in this chapter.

As children develop, it's entirely natural for them to look at and explore the bodies of other young children and compare the similarities and the differences. It's just as natural that they get at least some sexual pleasure from doing it. If they discover it, parents often forbid this activity and scold or punish the children. Again, they're wrong. All a child has to hear is that what he's doing is "naughty" and he'll try even harder to do whatever it is the parents are forbidding. There's extra excitement in doing something because it's forbidden. That's why children keep right on playing the childhood games they've always played— mama and papa, doctor and nurse—the same games the parents played, too, but have now conveniently forgotten. It's these games that children use to look at and explore each other's bodies.

Whether their parents tell them it's "naughty" or they hear the word from playmates, children aren't likely to tell their parents what they're doing. Consequently when parents discover that sex play is happening, they get upset and often blow the whole thing out of proportion. That's when the generation gap opens up for the first time. Unless something happens to change things, it won't be long before parents find themselves unable to talk openly to their children about sex. Meanwhile the children go on happily developing their sex lives, usually in a quite normal way —and in secret.

Parents don't seem to understand that there's nothing unusual or "dangerous" about early sex play. Much of the time it amounts to nothing more than looking at another child's sex organ. A girl may touch a boy's penis, and a boy may touch her vulva. It's a simple matter of exploring with the hands instead of the eyes. Sometimes very young boys and girls may try to have intercourse with each other, but usually there's no actual penetration by the penis. Most often the boy gets on top of the girl and goes through the motions. Children at this early stage rarely understand what actually happens in intercourse. Only a very few try to insert something into a girl's vagina—a finger or a stick—and even fewer try to put their mouths on another's sex organ.

For most girls, such early sex play produces no sexual arousal on their part. Maybe one out of ten gets a feeling she could identify in later years as arousal. For those few girls who are aroused, however, the experience can lead to orgasm, and it can be as full and complete and satisfying as those they'll have when they're older. Even baby girls less than a year old can have these orgasms, and sometimes they do.

Girls in general tend to have more sex play at younger ages, say from four to nine, than they do between ten and thirteen. For half the girls who experience early sex play, it happens only once, or perhaps two or three times at the most. For others it happens more often, and these experiences may cover the entire preadolescent period.

Girls sometimes have sex play with other girls—

about as often as with boys. This, too, is usually just curious exploration rather than any deliberate attempt at sexual arousal. For about a third of children, such episodes consist only of looking; the other two-thirds go so far as to touch, and in two out of ten cases, it involves the insertion of fingers or other objects into the vagina. That happens more frequently between girls than between boys and girls. These experiences between girls rarely involve oral-genital contact—that is, the mouth on the sex organ—and as I've noted, the same is true for boys.

On the whole, boys are more likely to have sex play before adolescence than girls. Not infrequently a girl may be involved in sex play with two or more boys at the same time, but fewer boys are ever involved with two or more girls simultaneously. It's true, too, that boys are more likely to start sex play with girls than the other way around.

All this sex play, either with boys or with girls, is usually exciting and pleasurable, but it can also be worthwhile in the sense that it helps later sexual adjustment. A few difficulties may complicate it, however. One is being found out by parents or other adults. In that case the experience is often exaggerated far beyond its simple and natural significance. Since most adults are convinced such behavior is wrong and dangerous, children are likely to be punished or made to feel unworthy or wicked, with consequent damage to their attitudes about sex.

Another difficulty stems from the first one. Since children involved in sex play often reflect adult attitudes about sex, if they know someone else has been caught doing it, they may ridicule the girl who's been found out, and her playmates may even shut her out of their circle—even if these accusers have been involved in sex play themselves.

Still another problem is the feeling of guilt some girls have whether they're caught or not. They realize that such play has to be kept secret, and they know it's disapproved of. That leads to feelings of being an outsider, of doing something terribly wrong, and a conviction that she's not worthwhile.

You've probably already gone through that part of your life, and however you reacted to it is now part of the past. But if you did have sex play as a child and felt guilty or unworthy about it, maybe you'll understand now that what you did was natural and shared by many other girls. You can have a positive attitude about it now and see what you thought was "bad" in a different light.

As I observed earlier, boys are much more specific in their sexual interests than girls, so it isn't surprising that older men are sometimes interested in young girls and hope to get some kind of sexual response from them. At least a quarter of girls reaching adolescence have been approached by older men or perhaps have even had direct sexual contact with them. By the time they're seventeen, nearly all girls have had approaches made to them in one way or another.

Such approaches are often harmless. Much as feminists may deplore it, appreciative whistles from strangers on the street or from passing truck drivers are trivial. The feminists argue that such behavior degrades women by making them sex objects, but this has been so through recorded history. But half-joking sexual advances from a girl friend's father may or may not be another matter. If he puts his arm around her from behind and presses on her breasts, or strokes her buttocks affectionately, or likes to put his arms around her, it may be a hardly concealed sexual advance.

It may be harder to deal with a loving uncle who pats his niece's thigh or some other part of her anatomy, and even more frequently, it may be a more or less direct sexual advance from a young father who is taking a baby-sitter home. Approaches can be verbal or they can go to the other extreme of exposing the penis or touching a girl's sex organ, or if a man gets the response he hopes for, actual intercourse.

Girls are often embarrassed and bewildered about how to handle these situations. Most likely they'll feel threatened and uncomfortable, at least, particularly since they've neither invited nor expected the advances. Or so they honestly believe. Yet sometimes a flirtatious girl, full of herself and conscious of her sexual attractiveness, may encourage a man without realizing she's done it.

If a girl is approached by an older man and hasn't invited it, the best thing to do is to let him know flatly, and at once, that she's not interested. There's no need to be hysterical. Just be firm. Otherwise, if she's hesitant and silent, so confused and taken aback that she doesn't know what to say or how to handle the situation, a man may take her silence for consent. The problem may be complicated, too, if a young girl feels that she's in the presence of a more powerful person, an authority figure like her parents, and thinks she can deal with him as she would a boy of her own age —probably the only similar experience she's ever had.

A girl should remember that she has every right to let the man know how she feels. Afterward she'll be much more careful not to let herself be put in such a situation again. Unfortunately, it can't always be anticipated. The advances of a girl friend's father, or the father of the baby you've been sitting with, are hard to anticipate unless there have been some previous warning signs. If something happens unexpectedly, it's right not to be awed by his greater age and authority and to simply reject his advance, just as you would those from a boy you didn't like well enough to let him fondle you.

It's the girl who consciously or unconsciously invites advances from older men who may be in trouble. Sometimes it's the sheer pleasure of knowing she can attract an older man, one who has singled her out, that makes her act in a flirtatious or a seductive way. That's when things get out of hand, because the man is likely to become more aggressive than a girl likes or knows how to handle.

What we've been talking about are things that can happen in everyday life. A different kind of problem is the "flasher," as we say, the stranger who exposes his penis to a young girl. These men have a serious psychological problem and can't help their compulsive behavior. Sometimes they mistakenly hope that a young girl may be interested, but often they want to see the reaction of shock, revulsion, or surprise. The best way to deal with them is to show complete indifference and keep cool. In such a situation a girl may think it's the exhibited penis that's ugly and repulsive, but in fact it's the circumstances surrounding the incident that are repellent, not the penis itself.

Another fairly common experience occurs when a girl goes to a movie alone, and a man sitting next to her slips a hand under her thigh or makes some other kind of sexual advance. Your response should be simple. Get up and move to another seat. If he persists, complain to the manager.

Society frowns on sex play between children, but then, society disapproves of a great many other sexual acts, and there are two sides to this story. It's true that sometimes there are good reasons for disapproval, but there is also a great deal of overreaction to sexual behavior that some people don't like. As I've said, a girl who has had sex play with girls and boys her own age is likely to have benefited from the experiences in one way or another, particularly her later adjustments to sex, and consequently they're valuable, even if some of them turned out badly. In that case she may learn as she would from any other unhappy experience. Otherwise, she will have learned something positive about the way her own body works, what its reactions can be, and something about other people, too. Pleasure has been given and received. All these things have their value for the future.

CHAPTER · 4

Getting to Know Boys

Eventually the time comes—early for some, later for others—when you'll be going out with boys. Often this new life begins with going to parties in a group or just "hanging out." But then you'll want to go out with one boy, to a movie or a concert or some place where the two of you can be together.

All this is an easy, pleasant learning experience, or it should be, one that paves the way to adult relationships, both sexual and nonsexual. That's the ideal. But as every teen-ager knows, there are few areas of boy-girl relationships where more problems arise. Parents and teachers know that, too, but the knowledge of pain and often heartache is what haunts the teen-ager.

Adults are likely to smile and dismiss this adolescent struggle. It's just part of growing up, they say; the kids will get over it. That may be true, but it doesn't mean the kids can't do anything about their problems. It's quite natural to be disturbed when these situations occur, and they do, but better understanding can improve any kind of human relationship. Going out is no exception.

One of the first things to understand is something I pointed out earlier. There's a great difference in the way boys and girls grow up at this stage of their lives, and that accounts for a large part of the trouble. Girls grow up faster than boys. That's the basic difficulty. Their height starts increasing rapidly a year or more before the boys begin to shoot up, and for thirteen- and fourteen-year-olds, this can be a potentially embarrassing situation.

A girl discovers that she's suddenly able to look over the head of the boy she's liked and played with since they were children. It may be two or three years before they're back on even terms. Meanwhile, human nature being what it is, girls may not want to go out with boys shorter than they are. On the flip side, many boys, just beginning to date about this time, find such discrimination hard to understand, even though they themselves may not feel comfortable going out with a taller girl. As a consequence of all this, younger girls who have begun to grow that much may find themselves going out with boys a little older than they are. But since other girls are late starters, or are naturally shorter, opportunities may even up.

More importantly, girls mature earlier than boys. Their pubic hair usually grows before the male's, and

their breasts get larger before
breast knots in a boy begin to swell
girls menstruate about a year before
ejaculate, but there's a reverse difference
has sperm in his semen from the beginning
girl probably won't produce egg cells capable
ization at the time of her first menstruation, and
we don't have absolute proof. It may take se
months, even years, before this ovulation process
gins. We do know, however, that such a delay isn't tru
of all girls.

You've already learned in an earlier chapter that an
important difference between boys and girls at this
stage is that most boys become suddenly intensely
interested in sex, but most girls don't. True, girls *are*
interested in boys in ways they haven't been before,
but they think of this new relationship in terms of
going out and having a good time, while boys are
sexually excited and feel an urge toward ejaculation,
even if it's unconscious. Since girls don't often know
how boys are feeling at this particular time, they're
frequently quite surprised to find out they've excited a
boy sexually by flirting with him or letting him fondle
her a little. A girl may have some romantic feelings
about him, but in most cases she thinks of this as just
another kind of friendship.

In spite of these and other difficulties, going out
together is something both sexes want to do. That
urge raises an old, old problem, best expressed in the
all too common question, "I like this boy, but I don't
know if he likes me. How can I get him to go out with

the corresponding
On the average,
boys are able to
e here. A boy
ing, while a
e of fertil-
though
veral
be-

57

ut are eager to start,
don't know how to

t in terms of going
clothes, you go to
thing with boys.
where the boys
y're shopping,
ay or not.

st place to look? Of course—in
re you're in daily contact with boys your
wn age, and the going-out process ordinarily begins
right there. If you go to a girls' school, it may be a little
more difficult, but these days school authorities aren't
as protective as they once were. They arrange frequent parties and other events to bring boys and girls
together.

School isn't the only place to meet boys. Young
people's groups in community clubs or churches are
good places, and so is the library. If your parents take
you on a summer vacation, opportunities are likely to
spring up like flowers. Summer jobs of all kinds, no
matter where they are, offer still more chances. A
more oblique approach is to choose girl friends who
are already going out. That often leads to meeting
friends of their friends.

Sometimes it's easy to meet boys and sometimes
it's hard, but in any case it's only the beginning. Some
girls who read this may have tried all the approaches
I've mentioned, and still they don't get chances to go
out. If that should happen to be your case, you don't

have to look very far for the cause. It's *you*, particularly your attitude toward yourself. If it's hard for other people, including boys, to like you, chances are it's because you don't like yourself.

Oddly enough, it's hard for some girls to understand that. They think, as many people do, that if other people demonstrate a liking for them, they'll automatically like themselves. But it's the other way around. Self-approval is a highly important element in living happily. It comes from a girl's view of herself, or a boy's of *himself*.

What does it really mean to "like yourself"? For one thing, it means not to be obsessed with whatever physical imperfections you may have. If you aren't absorbed in the fact that your teeth are slightly crooked, or that you have an abundance of freckles, or that your hair isn't the color you wish it was, or that your figure isn't as good as your friend's, then you're well on the way to liking yourself. Physical qualities alone don't make real beauty. Some of the most beautiful girls I've known would never be eligible for a beauty contest, let alone win one. On the other side of the coin, some beauty contest winners have had a hard time establishing satisfying relationships with men. Girls who think boys like only the prettiest girls are looking at the wrong boys. Those who seem to be hung up on beauty usually turn out to be not the kind you'd like to go out with.

There are a good many aspects of a girl's relationship with herself that can get in the way of going out successfully. Some girls have personality problems, like those who are in such a state of extreme rebellion at home that this situation has become the most important thing in their lives. Others may be in constant conflict with their brothers and sisters, and that, too, absorbs their emotions. Still others have strong guilt feelings about things they may have done in the past, and the result has been to erect a high wall between them and the rest of the world. Then of course there are the truly lonely girls, most of them painfully shy. All the kinds of girls I've mentioned here are going to have serious problems finding boys to go out with.

The effect of personality problems is to make a girl so concerned with herself and her problems that she can't see a boy as an individual in his own right, a human being with his own feelings and desires. She sees him and everything else around her only in relation to herself. That's what I mean when I say girls have to like themselves before other people will like *them*. That doesn't mean being egotistical; it just means they have to believe they're as good as anybody else.

I can hear you saying, "How do I *start* liking myself?" I'll have to admit there's no easy answer to that question, and I won't pretend there is. But one thing I'm certain of. Any girl can make a start simply by recognizing that she's going to be much happier if she understands that something needs to be done, and begins to make an inventory of her own personality to see where she needs to change.

It's strange, but some girls have a lot of difficulty recognizing the most self-evident things about themselves. Pretty girls often deny they're pretty, and are even embarrassed when someone tells them they are. They need to accept the fact that they're attractive, and make the most of their natural charm, because it will take them far in all kinds of relationships. Far more common are those girls who are convinced they're *not* attractive. It often turns out, however, that they've realized they're not as attractive physically as some other girl they're comparing themselves with. They should realize that few girls look like movie stars. They put themselves down on the basis of something completely superficial. Plenty of girls who aren't pretty, or even reasonably good-looking, are sought after by boys because they're such good and interesting company, or because they have sparkling personalities, or for a lot of other reasons that have nothing to do with conventional beauty.

If you want to start learning how to like yourself, begin by deciding what your best points are, and work on developing them even further. At the same time be honest with yourself. Maybe you have some bad points, too, or at least characteristics that set you apart from other girls (or boys). They can be overcome with a little work. You may be shy, for example, and that can create social problems. But don't despair; even shyness can be conquered if you work at it. If you can't express yourself very well, that isn't hard to cure, either. Perhaps you realize, if someone hasn't told you, that you have a short temper, and that's a trait you can eliminate if you try.

But after you've faced your bad qualities and done

something about them, the most important thing is to focus on your *good* qualities. Learn to think well of yourself because you have them, and you'll find that your relations with other people will improve. Remember that people change all through their lives, and at any point they can change themselves if they want to do so badly enough. It takes honesty, determination, and work.

As teen-agers know, it's the feeling of rejection that lies at the bottom of many of their difficulties. If your father, mother, or someone else rejects you, or if you think they do, it may or may not be true, but in any case it doesn't mean you deserve to be rejected or that other people feel the same way. In fact, it may be just the opposite. Boys won't reject a girl just because she won't do *everything* they want her to. It's much better to be independent, to be your own self.

Girls realize today that boys and marriage, or some other kind of living together, aren't the only options available. You need to think about what you're going to do with your nonsexual life—and that means most of it. Even so, it's true that if you're able to relate well to boys in going out with them during adolescence, and that includes having the right image of yourself, it will help you relate to the men you'll be involved with later on, both in and out of the business or professional world. Especially your intimate relations with them, whether it's marriage or living with someone. The way to learn how to have good relationships with males is by doing what you have to do in learning anything else—practice. How to relate to another person—and in general how to be a responsive individual —takes a lot of practice and self-knowledge.

But let's assume now that you don't have any personality problems of consequence and you don't have any problem meeting boys. The next most common question is when to start going out, and that is likely to generate conflict with parents. Both girls and parents often aren't sure when is the best time to begin, or even whether there is a "best" time.

The answer seems too simple to be true. The right time is when a girl *feels* that it's the right time. First of all, going out is a matter of two people pairing off so they can get to know each other better, or simply for companionship. In the background, however, especially in the minds of parents, is the fact that one is male and the other female, and that may lead to some kind of physical contact and some kind of emotional relationship based on feelings that are more than simple friendship.

When I say the "right time," I mean the time when a girl thinks she's ready to develop a boy-girl relationship with potential. For a boy the potential is probably sexual, whether he admits it or not. He will be thinking about kissing, fondling, maybe intercourse. For a girl the potential is to be liked and accepted—singled out as a special person. Moreover, going out means that a boy is interested enough in her to take her places, and that gives her a sense of her own importance, a sense of status.

But the beginning of going out may also be the beginning of a conflict with parents, as I've said earlier. The tension rises from the fact that when a girl feels she's ready to go out, chances are her parents will think it's too early. That creates a real problem—whether to disobey the parents or wait until they permit it.

All this is a nearly inevitable part of growing up, and it can be hard on both parents and children. If they think hard enough about the conflict, it should be clear to children that the real issue is responsibility. Parents want to feel their girls and boys are going to behave responsibly when they're away from home in a new situation. If a girl demonstrates that she's responsible in smaller things, there may be less objection to her going out.

If you have this problem, and you find it impossible to discuss it calmly and sensibly with your parents, or if they're simply adamant about not letting you go out, you may well go out anyway, and lie about it—the worst circumstances. You'll have to sneak around instead of enjoying this new experience easily and naturally. That may be the first time a girl has to confront her parents on the whole question of honesty about something fundamental. If you're in this situation, I hope you'll examine your own set of values carefully and try to decide whether it's more important to be honest with parents or do what the other girls are doing. It's too bad, but both courses have their drawbacks, and you'll have to face those honestly, too.

In the end, it comes down to a question of obeying parents and giving up temporarily some of the things you want to do—things the other girls are doing—or going ahead and suffering guilt feelings, always with the fear of being caught in the back of your mind. It takes real guts, but sometimes a girl may be further ahead if she simply asserts her independence and refuses to go along with the others simply because "everybody's doing it." That kind of independence won't start you on going out, but it may earn you some respect and admiration.

Girls who have problems with parents over going out, or over boyfriends if they do go out, need some older person they can talk to. That someone shouldn't be a moralizer, or one given to judgments, but someone who'll just listen and understand. A girl is lucky if she has such parents. If not, a teacher may help sometimes, or a guidance counselor, or a loved relative. I'm not suggesting here that this older person is wiser or knows better. I only mean that such a person, simply by listening sympathetically, can help a girl clarify problems in her own mind—another way of helping her feel better about herself.

But now let's assume that you don't have any of these problems, and that you're already happily going out with boys. Either they're calling you for dates, or sometimes you're calling one of them. That last wouldn't have been considered a good thing to do twenty years ago, when I first wrote this book. Today it's taken for granted that a girl has every right to ask a boy if he wants to go out somewhere. There's nothing aggressive about it, just a sharing of mutual interests. If there's something you want to do or see, and you know a boy who would be likely to want the same thing, it's now easy enough to talk to him about it and say, "Let's go there together" or "I heard this new club is really great—why don't we go and try it?"

So one way or another you're going out. The next big question is whether to go out in the other sense—to go steady, as we used to say. There's always been a question about whether this is a good idea or not, and even with changing times, the debate is far from over. In fact, if there's one subject in a girl's sexual and social development where advice is superabundant, this is it.

As always, there's something to be said on both sides. A girl who goes out all the time with one boy has a welcome sense of security. That is, wherever she wants to go, she always has someone to go with, and she won't have any lonely evenings. But then there's also the fact that going steady permits a deeper emotional relationship to develop, and that can have all kinds of consequences, some only momentarily painful, others more serious.

There *is* something to be said for going out with a good many boys. If she does, a girl will have a better chance to find out what kind of male she wants to live with eventually, if that's what she intends to do. She'll discover what personality traits in a boy attract her and which make her unhappy. She may find out that moody, irritable boys don't suit her easygoing, essentially optimistic way of looking at things. Or she finds that boys with sharp tempers frighten her. Or that sloppy boys get on her nerves if she's inclined toward neatness—or the other way around. She'll be able to see clearly the difference between an uncaring person and one who's warm and loving. Such experiences help a girl make up her mind later about what kind of person she chooses to share her life with, and it may save her from bad and risky situations.

It wouldn't be realistic, however, to say that girls necessarily wind up having relationships with the kind of men who are best for them. As often as not the reverse is true, and some girls appear to have a talent for being involved with men who are going to make them unhappy. But it's also true that early and varied experiences can affect the later choice of deep relationships in a positive way.

Another advantage of playing the field is that a girl will be in a far greater variety of social situations, meeting new parents, making new friends, and that is all good experience in learning how to construct a satisfactory social life, besides being satisfying in itself.

There's one very real danger in going steady. Every girl who reads this has almost certainly heard about it from someone, but it's worth repeating. It's the fact that many of those who begin going steady early wind up marrying either while they're still in high school or just after graduation. This is the group that has the highest divorce rate. A few years after marriage, both partners often realize that there are a lot of other people in the world, and a great many other experiences, both sexual and otherwise, that they've missed by settling so early for one person. A substantial part of the precious freedom that is the particular property of the young has gone and won't come back.

These young couples, still in their early twenties and usually with one or more children, often feel themselves trapped, and many hasten to get themselves untrapped. People can make a new start with a divorce, certainly, but there's often the problem of the children (men are not in a hurry to marry a divorced woman with children, although many do), and in any case, it isn't psychologically easy to start all over again. And starting over at a later stage in life can be difficult.

Patterns in going out today are likely to follow a mixed course. Girls (and boys, too) don't seem to choose between going steady and playing the field; they alternate periods of close, steady friendship with one person, followed by going out with several boys.

When you do go out, the chief questions that arise concern behavior, and here the differences between the sexes become really important. Even in the new liberated era, girls are more concerned about their reputations than boys are. How far they'll go in letting a boy fondle them, for example, is often determined more by what the boy is going to tell other boys than by anything else.

When a boy starts to kiss a girl, he imagines or hopes that she'll be thinking, "Isn't this great? What have I been waiting for?" Instead, if he only knew, she's likely to be thinking, "I wonder what he'll think of me," or, "Will he tell the other boys, and what will *they* think?" That doesn't always happen, of course, and many couples plunge into this kind of lovemaking without any thoughts at all except having fun. But the social system still plays the mindless game of "good girl'' and "bad girl," so the best thing a girl can do is to have confidence in herself and in the way she relates to her own world. If she does this, she may not get involved in sexual situations before she's emotionally ready for them.

I think it makes more sense for a girl to decide rationally how far she wants to go in a particular situation with a particular boy, rather than to be concerned about her reputation. I know it's hard to be rational when you're emotionally involved, but there's no easy solution. A girl has to think about it or not think about it. At least she should understand she has a clear choice.

Certainly there should be a better reason to guide a girl in how far she should go than what other people might think. Some girls go further than they want to because they're afraid the boy will tell other boys that they're "frigid" or "prudish."

It's a handicap for a girl to be always involved in her own problems, and similarly it's just as crippling for her to be always concentrating on her "reputation." A girl wants to have the freedom to be interested in what interests the boy she's going out with, but she can do that only if she's free of her own hangups. The old gag line goes, "Let's talk about *you* for a while. What do *you* think of me?" Far too many girls behave just like that. A girl should never do that, not only when she's out with a boy, but when she's with anybody. That's what bores are made of. People don't want to hear about the state of your health, unless there's something really serious going on, nor about your hair problems, or your experiences with other boys. Any girl could add to that list, and boys could make it longer.

It's a problem of communicating, of being able to express feelings whether they're positive or negative, and the ability to respond to the feelings others express. Communicating means more than just talking, though. For instance, a girl can *talk* about a coming school dance, but she *communicates* her feelings about going to it. Communicating feelings is more dangerous, because then a girl makes herself more vulnerable, more open. Yet the stubborn thing about it is that a good relationship with another person, boy or girl, involves exactly this openness and danger. I'm talking about a kind of communication that's honest and sincere, not worrying about its effect on the other person. In short, a girl should be herself—natural, open, not exclusively concerned with making an impression on others.

Girls can help boys in this respect. Boys often fail to understand the role they should play in boy-girl relationships. All kinds of small social gestures go with relationships, and people are unfortunately prone to forget them these days. Boys have seen too many *Rambo* tough-guy movies, for example. I'm not talking about perpetuating old conventions between the sexes, but about courtesy to another human being. Many girls and women still appreciate it, even in the new age of equality, if a boy helps a girl on with her coat—or vice versa—or opens a car door, or carries her books if they're obviously a heavy load.

It isn't a question of right or wrong. A girl who subtly encourages a boy to remember these little things is emphasizing in another way the boy-girl relationship. That's what going out is all about. By helping a boy observe these ancient and supposedly outdated customs, a girl helps to develop the male-female bond between them that she wants to establish.

There's another problem in going out, and it can be a serious one. That's the problem of age difference. Girls often want to know how much older a boy can be and still be an acceptable person to go out with. There's no simple answer, obviously. For example, a boy's actual age may be far different from his emotional age—up or down. A girl often finds it gratifying to have the attention of an older boy, or even a man, because it makes her feel more special.

Here, for instance, is a thirteen-year-old girl who's going out with a high school junior or senior. That can be a worthwhile relationship if it's based on common interests and mutual attraction. But it will help this girl, and perhaps save her from trouble, if she asks herself what other reasons the older boy might have for taking her out. Is he emotionally mature? Is he thinking of her only as a possible sexual conquest because she's exceptionally attractive, even though she's so much younger? If the answer to any of these questions is yes, a girl may want to reconsider going out with him, even though she's excited about such flattering attention.

As the age difference increases, so do the problems. Here's the same girl, but this time she's going out with a twenty-one-year-old boy who's just back from college on vacation, or maybe he's out of school and working. Certainly it's possible for two such people to have a good and meaningful relationship, but now the odds are more heavily against it. The same questions should be asked, particularly the one about his emotional maturity.

There's an even longer step this hypothetical girl might take, one that would apply more to a girl who's older. She may be going out secretly with the thirty-five-year-old father of the baby she sits with. Even this relationship could be a positive one, but the odds are so heavily against it that it's much more reasonable to expect disastrous consequences. Of course, it's exciting and fun to be noticed by such a man, but it appears to be true that the greater the age difference, the greater the chance that the older man will have some psychological problem that leads him into such a relationship. A girl's interests are likely to be different from his, and the relationship is almost certain to end badly.

Going out with married men of any age, and particularly falling in love with one, is an invitation to trouble and heartbreak. Smart girls know that no matter what such a man may tell her, or how convincingly he says it, the odds are at least a thousand to one that he won't divorce his wife and marry the girl. Neither his love for the girl nor whatever unhappiness he may have at home is likely to be a decisive factor when the crunch comes, as it inevitably will. To go through the agony of divorce, often with the wife fighting it, is too much for a man to contemplate in most cases. That's something his teen-age girl friend won't understand.

A girl who finds herself in this situation shouldn't deceive herself about the outcome or about the man involved. If she's willing to put up with empty weekends, surreptitious meetings, and having only part of a man, then she's entitled to whatever short-range satisfaction she can get.

Every situation is different, I know, and special. The girl who's dating a married man believes firmly that in her case the odds are much more in her favor than they really are. But if only she can stop deceiving herself long enough to examine her situation honestly, she may discover that things are different from what she thought. If she's able to talk openly and freely to someone who's not directly involved with her life, it will help her see the situation more clearly.

Of all the questions a counselor hears from young girls, I suppose the most frequent is the plaintive query: "How do I know I'm in love?"

First of all, love isn't sex alone. They're separate things, although they may occur together. A girl loves her parents or her dog or her best friend without the involvement of sex. On the other hand, it's possible to have sex with someone you don't love. Many times love and sexual feelings are part of the same response, and when that combination occurs, it can be one of the most profound and meaningful experiences human beings are capable of having.

Being "in love" isn't something distinct and separate from being "not in love." If we put it on a scale, the range would be from zero to a hundred. At one end would be the feelings a girl has for a boy she likes and sometimes goes out with. As she knows him better and they go out more often, her feelings move upward on the scale until the time comes when she feels warm and excited just being with him, wants to be with him as much as possible, and would rather be with him than anyone else. At that point, a girl could say with some confidence, "I'm in love."

That doesn't mean she's reached the opposite end of the scale. There may be a distance to go, perhaps, and since love isn't exactly a fixed and stable emotion, she may go up and down the scale for a time. Affection may be followed by sexual feelings and a depth of emotion far from what it was at the beginning. If it was only "puppy love," it would never have gone so far. Such love comes quickly and goes quickly, no matter how painful it may seem at the time.

At the far end of the scale is love, real love, solid and unmistakable. It's based on trust, understanding, consideration, and open communication, and it's very much worth having.

I've been talking in these pages about the sexual aspects of a girl's life, because that's what the book is about. But I hope no girl who reads it will underestimate the importance of love or fail to see that sex is only one of the many faces of love. It's possible to have sex without love and love without sex, but it's the blending of the two that produces one of the most satisfying and rewarding of human experiences.

A girl's sexual feelings for a boy may not lead to intercourse, until she thinks she's ready for it, but those feelings become important only as they reinforce her total feeling of commitment, trust, and understanding—in a word, love.

CHAPTER · 5

Going Out

We've been talking about the problems involved in starting to go out; now let's look at what happens (and doesn't happen) when you *do* go out. The most important thing to think about is what you do sexually with a boy. That's particularly important now, with the menace of AIDS to consider. You may not be ready for sexual contact involving penetration, but it's not too early these days to learn about condoms and how they're used, as well as the nature of AIDS itself, which I'll explain in a later chapter. Let's consider, then, what might happen if you're alone with a boy and sex is in the air.

First of all, of course, there's kissing. It comes in a good many varieties. Very young girls kiss with lips closed and rather tight. When they kiss a boy they're out with, it may not be much different to them from the way they'd kiss anybody else. Eventually, however, if there's sexual arousal, the lips open and move and tongues are mutually inserted in the other's mouth. Once this was known as "soul kissing," or even more often, the "French kiss." (The French kiss the way everyone else does.) Today it's simply "tongue kissing," and that's exactly what it is.

If a girl does this with a boy, it probably means she's sexually aroused, because otherwise she would probably find it at least messy if not distasteful.

Tongue kissing, and any other physical contact of a sexual nature, comes under the general heading of "fondling," the most convenient word for it. Whatever takes place is a way of communicating sexual feelings to another person, but it can't have much, if any, meaning unless the feelings are mutual. Consequently, if a girl can't accept the feeling a boy is trying to communicate to her, she is better off to discourage whatever's happening. She should know, too, that a boy may be so aroused himself that he forgets about her response completely and doesn't care whether she's responding or not. That's the time to cut it off—gently and diplomatically, if possible, but completely in any case.

Mutual fondling ought to involve at least some degree of affection and emotional feeling. Both the girl and the boy should be interested in and appreciate the other person. But a girl needs to understand that this is also a prelude to intercourse and almost always precedes it. We call it "foreplay." In fondling, the implication of intercourse is always there, and a girl should be aware of this and govern herself accordingly.

Like so many aspects of early sexuality, fondling is a learning experience. It progresses from one step to another, and the progress can be stopped at any point. In its simplest form, it consists of hugging someone warmly—a universal gesture of affection that everyone needs, whether the intent is sexual or not. Hugging is the most common demonstration of affection in our society.

The next step is kissing. If a girl has never kissed a boy, as I suggested earlier, she finds these first kisses a little awkward and probably not very exciting, except for the knowledge that she's doing it. It takes sexual excitement to make her lips go soft and open up, so that tongue kissing almost inevitably follows.

From there, fondling usually proceeds to the boy's putting a hand on a girl's breast outside her clothing, then inside, and sometimes touching the breast with his lips. It's only a short step from that point to putting his hand on her sex organ, and she may do that to him as well, first outside the clothing, then inside. If intercourse is going to follow, a boy may put his mouth on the girl's sex organ, or they may do this together at the same time—what we call "69," for obvious reasons when you study the figures.

Until the advent of AIDS, this was a kind of sexual activity widely practiced, even though it is forbidden by law in some states. Now, however, everyone including teen-agers needs to remember than one of the ways the AIDS virus is transferred is through the exchange of semen or vaginal secretions, and since no kind of protection is available in the case of "69," the risk is great if either partner carries the AIDS virus.

Fondling is such a common, happy experience that it hardly needs to be justified. It's a pleasurable experience that not only creates exciting body sensations but may lead to orgasm. People everywhere in the world enjoy this wonderful feeling. Another advantage is that if it stops short of intercourse, there's no danger of pregnancy unless a boy ejaculates at the opening of the vagina and the sperm work their way through the entire length of that organ and up into the uterus. The odds are long that this will happen, but it *can* occur. Still another advantage of fondling is that the possibility of communicating a venereal disease is remote, although infection is possible if there's mouth-genital contact.

Fondling may be better than intercourse itself as a learning experience for later relationships. A boy learns how to stimulate a girl, and the girl discovers what it's like to be stimulated. Because fondling embraces such a variety of contacts, from kissing to mouth-genital behavior, it can be learned in gradual steps. Every new step can be assimilated and become part of a girl's emotional knowledge—of herself and of boys.

Some people have argued in the past that fondling is harmful because it might fix a girl at this level and so prevent her from enjoying intercourse later, but unless there are psychological problems that prevent a girl from enjoying intercourse, there's no truth in this. Such problems aren't caused by fondling experiences.

A girl may not particularly like fondling when she first begins and will most likely go slowly. But as she learns to like it, progressing from one step to another, she must remember that the boy will want to go much faster than she does, and she'll have to make him slow down. Of course, this isn't always true. It depends a lot on the girl's background and her emotional nature. If she *does* want to go slowly, however, she should explain to the boy, gently, how she feels, and if he cares enough about her as a person, he'll respect her feelings.

Girls find out quickly that boys want to go as far as they're permitted. Some girls use this fact as a kind of lever for bargaining, whether they do it consciously or unconsciously. If a boy has been especially attentive and taken her to an especially nice place, a girl may allow him to go further than she would otherwise. But if she feels she's been shortchanged on an evening out, she may refuse him anything more than a good-night kiss, if that.

I'm not in favor of this kind of emotional blackmail. It's too manipulative for its own good. I'm sure you've heard a girl say, "What did he expect for a lousy hamburger and a cup of coffee?" That's exactly the wrong attitude. Fondling with a boy isn't an exchange of favors, giving something in proportion to what's given to you. It's an exchange of mutual feelings, and nothing else ought to be involved.

A girl who feels hostile or irritated about

something may sometimes deliberately let a boy get aroused and then refuse to continue. It's her way of punishing him. I'm sure you'll understand that using sex in this manner, as a weapon, not only is unfair but closes off any chance of establishing the kind of open communication that makes a relationship desirable.

It's hard for a young and inexperienced girl to understand how much more sexually oriented boys are than she is. Since that's so, she may often say or do provocative things that will be constantly frustrating to a boy, without understanding what she's doing. It will be doubly frustrating if some fondling doesn't occur. This situation can happen as a result of an unintended double meaning. For example, a girl may say at the end of an evening, "My parents are in bed. Come on in and we'll have a good time."

What she's thinking of is listening to some music, perhaps, or having something to eat in the kitchen. But a boy hearing such a remark translates it instantly as "The coast is clear and we can have some sex." When he finds out that what he thinks is an open invitation turns out to be something else, he has probably already tried to fondle the girl and is astonished to find her shocked and resisting. Astonished and no doubt angry, too, he goes home both mad and frustrated.

In another situation, after a long kiss during a fondling session, a girl may say, "I'm hot!" The boy translates this as "I'm aroused and ready to go" and accordingly tries to take the next step. He can't believe it when he finds out she meant it literally. *She's* surprised to think that anyone could misinterpret so innocent a remark. Again, girls need to remember how much more sexually oriented boys are and should exercise a little caution with their vocabularies.

Boys have a short, descriptive word for girls who they think get them deliberately worked up and then back off, leaving them frustrated. The word is "cockteaser," accurate but ugly. It describes a kind of behavior that's clearly unfair, one that tells us something about the personality of the girl who does it. With some girls it may be unconscious behavior. They don't understand what they're doing, or what effect it's having, because of their inexperience and ignorance. They're surprised and indignant when a boy responds aggressively to being treated that way. The only solution to this problem is information. If a girl is told what her behavior is causing, she'll probably stop doing it.

There *are* girls, of course, who know perfectly well what they're doing, and keep on doing it out of malice, spite, or resentment—the result of psychological problems. Such a girl becomes an actress playing the lead role in a drama of hostility; her actions are inspired by deep-seated and complicated feelings that have made her dislike males in general. This is how she gets even with them.

Then there are a few who tease for an entirely different reason. Other girls have told them it's the smart thing to do, and they may even describe in detail how to do it. And finally, in still another category are those girls who simply want to dominate males. They tease because it's a way of controlling boys and showing their aggression.

Returning now to girls who *like* fondling, it can be said that those who do it to orgasm are doing themselves a favor. Generally speaking, if they have orgasm when they're young, they'll have an easier time making good sexual adjustments when they're adults. Of all the ways to have orgasm, fondling to that point is probably the most helpful. If a girl is aroused sexually and doesn't have an orgasm, however, it can leave her feeling frustrated and unsatisfied. If this experience occurs again and again, it builds up habit patterns difficult to break in later life.

Fondling without orgasm may also leave a girl with pains in her groin, just as it does with boys, and they can be very uncomfortable. About half the girls aroused during fondling have that experience, and about a third of them masturbate afterward to relieve tension—again, just as boys do. To continue fondling until orgasm occurs or to masturbate later are certainly better ways to live than to put up with frustration and uneasiness.

Girls (parents, too) ought not to overemphasize fondling. Even in the present climate of freedom, there are still some girls who haven't experienced fondling before they graduate from high school, although the number is probably diminishing. Many, probably most, don't start until they're thirteen or fourteen, but begin in their early teens. Comparatively few enter adult life without ever having done it.

Fondling to the point of orgasm is much more

common now than it used to be, and chances are it will continue to increase unless some kind of backlash occurs, which scarcely seems likely. For girls who aren't ready for intercourse, it solves the problem of learning how to respond sexually to boys, which is important for them to know. Fondling and self-masturbation are probably the most acceptable kinds of sexual behavior among adolescent girls.

Behavior patterns obviously continue to change, however. There may be only a little more actual sexual behavior in this generation than in the previous one, but it's true that teen-agers drink more alcohol today, and as everyone knows, their use of drugs, particularly crack, has become a national problem.

Boys sometimes get the mistaken idea that alcohol is the best way to stimulate a girl to sex. They imagine that they themselves are more alert and sensitive to every kind of stimulation when they drink (even though the opposite is true) and are convinced that all boys and girls can drink themselves into sex.

In a way, that's true. Alcohol *does* remove some inhibitions. But it's a depressant, not a stimulant, and it takes only a drink or two to depress the higher nervous centers. Some inhibition is lost, and the illusion of being stimulated occurs. But then it takes only a little more to depress the lower nervous centers, with quite a different effect. Then the drinker won't be able to function as well, sexually or otherwise, as he did before. The more he drinks, the longer it takes a boy to have an erection and ejaculate. As for the girl, the more she drinks, the less likely she'll be to *want* sex.

In all drugs, there are two broad categories. One includes depressants, like alcohol, and the other is stimulants. Marijuana, for example, is a depressant. The popular belief that "pot and sex" are inseparable is as much of a delusion as the belief about alcohol. If a stimulant drug is taken, all the way from amphetamines to crack, the effect is the same, oddly enough. These drugs stimulate the individual every way but sexually and have a depressing effect on sexual behavior. Mainline drugs like heroin knock out the taker sexually, and the user is completely unable to perform under their influence, although there may be elaborate sexual fantasies that lead users to believe they actually had great sex while they were under the influence.

Boys and girls should both understand that alcohol and drugs are like crutches as far as sex is concerned. If people think they need them to have sex, there's something wrong that can't be corrected without professional counseling. Sex exists by itself, fully and beautifully, without any artificial help.

CHAPTER · 6

What an Orgasm Is— and Isn't

Orgasm is one of those things that a good many women worry about unnecessarily. The novelist Mary McCarthy once called this perennial anxiety "the tyranny of the orgasm." Young girls aren't as likely to worry about it, since most of them won't experience it before they're fifteen, but they will during the next five years, in one way or another. That's too bad. There should be no problems about orgasm that healthy attitudes or good counseling can't solve.

It's quite natural, however, for girls to be curious about the orgasm, since in these days they read and hear so much about it. They want to know, "What's it really like? How will I feel? How do I know when I'm having it?"

Many of the great writers of world literature have tried to answer those questions, and modern novels are full of less masterful descriptions. Doctors have long since described its clinical aspects. Sometimes specialists in sexual studies are able, in a way, to combine the clinical with the literary. One famous sex researcher, Havelock Ellis, whose *Studies in the Psychology of Sex* was a pioneering landmark in the field, described orgasm achieved in intercourse as a state in which "the individual, as a separate person, tends to disappear. He has become one with another person, as nearly one as the conditions of existence ever permit."

Describing how a woman feels when she's having orgasm, Ellis speaks of her as having a "feeling of relieved tension and agreeable repose—a moment when, as one woman expresses it, together with intense pleasure, there is, as it were, a floating up into a higher sphere . . . [After the orgasm] there is a sensation of repose and self-assurance, and often an accession of free and joyous energy. . . . She may experience a feeling of intoxication that is followed by no evil reaction."

Such modern researchers as Masters and Johnson, whose studies of orgasm are a modern high-water mark in sex research, would never put it in such a flowery way, but their descriptions come down to the same thing, as do those of other researchers.

As a result of present-day studies, we now have a fairly comprehensive knowledge of what happens to the body during orgasm. It can be divided into four parts, of which the orgasm itself is the third. First there is the excitement phase, beginning with a moistening of the vagina by its lubricating fluid. This occurs in ten to thirty seconds from the first sexual stimulation, no matter what its source may be. Stimulation of the clitoris contributes to this phase, too, although it isn't essential. The nipples on the breasts become erect, and the breasts themselves increase in size. At the same time, the outer lips of the vulva, the labia majora, open a little, while the inner lips also tend to swell. Aside from the sex organs, this phase is also reflected in other parts of the body as the voluntary muscles tense, the pulse rate increases, blood pressure rises, and a rosy glow called the "sex flush" appears on the skin.

Excitement is succeeded by the plateau phase, although it would be hard to say where one phase stops and the next begins. Now the breathing rate increases. Pulse rate and blood pressure begin to rise. The sex flush becomes more marked and widespread, while muscle tension is heightened and the area around the breast nipples swells. Even more dramatic is the swelling of the tissues around the outer third of the vagina so that the diameter of the opening is reduced as much as 50 percent, enabling it to grip the penis. Other changes continue in the uterus and vagina. The uterus itself is enlarged, doubling in size in women who have had children. The clitoris elevates, like a male's erection, and the inner lips change in color from pink to bright red. This color change signals that an orgasm is going to occur in a minute or a little more if stimulation continues.

Orgasm itself is the third phase. There's a feeling of intense pleasure as the outer third of the vaginal tube goes into rhythmic muscular contractions, coming four-fifths of a second apart, until the intensity tapers off. In a mild orgasm, there may be only three to five contractions; in an intense one, eight to twelve. The uterus also contracts rhythmically, in wavelike motions, just as it does during childbirth, but these contractions aren't felt.

Other muscles may contract in the same way, while in the rest of the body, pulse rate, blood pressure, and breathing rate reach their peaks, the sex flush is pronounced, and all the body's muscles respond in some way. Even hands and feet contract in a spasm. Through it all, both male and female are unaware of these muscular exertions, and unless they know better, are surprised when their muscles ache next day.

After orgasm a kind of final resolution occurs. Swelling around the nipples subsides, giving the illusion that they are more erect than ever. This is a sure sign that a woman has really experienced orgasm. The sex flush disappears rapidly, and in many females a filmy sheen of perspiration appears on the body. In five or ten seconds the clitoris returns to its normal position, but it may take five or ten minutes, or as long as a half hour, to get back to normal size. The vagina relaxes, too, the uterus shrinks, and the cervix descends to its normal position. At this point, the passage through the cervix enlarges, making it easier for the sperm cells to swim into the uterus. It may be a half hour or more before a girl's body returns to the state it was in before she was stimulated. If she's reached the plateau stage without orgasm, it will take much longer —an hour, or even several hours.

Orgasms vary, just like the people who have them. For some girls it's a very mild experience, not much more than a sigh; or it can go to the opposite extreme and result in a state of ecstasy where her body thrashes about, with a momentary loss of awareness. It can last only a few seconds, or for thirty seconds and longer. In short, there's no right or wrong way to have an orgasm.

A common misconception, argued about for decades even to the present moment, is that there are two kinds of orgasm, one achieved by stimulating the clitoris, therefore called a clitoral orgasm, and the other a "vaginal orgasm," accomplished by the penis's penetration of the vagina. The first kind was thought to be achieved by masturbation, fondling, or intercourse if the male pubic area pressed against the clitoris. This was considered by some to be an immature kind of orgasm, related to early sexual experiences. Vaginal orgasms were believed to be more mature, the ultimate sexual experience for a woman.

Those ideas are no longer considered true. In intercourse, it's the stimulation of the clitoris by the male area above the penis that brings an orgasm in conjunction with pulling down the labia by the penis's action as it moves in and out of the vagina. That in turn stimulates the clitoris because the pulling-down action creates a hood of flesh over the sensitive tip of the clitoris, rubbing against it.

In fact, there's no real difference in the kind of orgasms girls have, whether by masturbation, fondling, or intercourse. It simply isn't true that if a girl has sex in one particular way—let's say masturbation—she won't be able to have orgasm any other way.

No matter how long it lasts or how intense it is, orgasm is an experience so specific and unique that when a girl has one, she'll be in no doubt that she's having it. In one way, it's like doing something more familiar—sneezing. If you still have doubts about whether you've had one or not after reading the description of orgasm I've just given, chances are good that you haven't.

There are several sources of orgasm. For young girls up to fifteen, most are produced (in those who have them) by self-masturbation. I'll talk about that in more detail later on. Dreams are another source, but only about two girls out of a hundred achieve orgasm that way at fifteen. By the time they're twenty, this figure increases to eight out of a hundred. At fifteen, three girls out of a hundred have had orgasm by being fondled to the point of climax, but again a dramatic change occurs in the next five years. At twenty, nearly 25 percent of girls who have orgasm achieve it this way while only 6 percent of girls have had orgasm from intercourse at fifteen. The figure rises to 11 percent between fifteen and twenty. An even smaller number, 2 percent, have had orgasm with other girls at fifteen, and at twenty this figure has risen by only a single percentage point.

Reading this, you might get the idea that everybody is engaged in some kind of sexual activity all the time, and if you've never had intercourse, you may be wondering why there's so much fuss about orgasm. After all, it may be a pleasurable experience to be enjoyed later, but there's no reason to get upset if you're not having it now. That's understandable. But there *is* something to be said for those who do have orgasm early. The longer a girl delays experiencing it, whatever the source, the more difficult it may be to have it in later life. A steady buildup of inhibition is likely to be taking place in the meantime.

That's a truth some parents may not like to hear. Yet it's a demonstrable fact that girls who have orgasm when they're young—that is, up to fifteen—are those who experience the least difficulty having it later on. It doesn't matter how the orgasm comes, whether it's from intercourse, being fondled, or masturbation. Half the girls who've never known what it's like to have an orgasm until they're married or enter into some other relationship fail to have one during the first year of that relationship, whatever it may be. Of those who *have* experienced it, only one in ten fails to have it in circumstances of regular intimacy.

Surprisingly, girls who have intercourse when they're young but still don't experience orgasm have just as hard a time, or harder, having it when they're established in a regular relationship, whether it's marriage or not. Clearly, a girl who learns what orgasm is at an early point in her adolescence is going to have a more fulfilling time later on.

We need to dispose right here of a superstition still earnestly believed by some people, that if a girl learns to have orgasms by masturbating herself, or having someone else do it to her, she'll be so accustomed to this method that she'll have trouble experiencing it in intercourse. There's no truth whatever in this notion. In fact, it's easier to transfer the way you achieve orgasm from one kind of sexual behavior to another than it is to have one in the first place.

Girls have one advantage over boys where the orgasm is concerned. It's their ability to have many of them in succession. While some young boys are able to have three or four in relatively quick succession, with a short interval between, they lose that ability progressively as they grow older. Many girls, on the other hand, are able to have an almost unlimited number in succession from the time of their first experience until their sexual activity ceases. That isn't true of all of them. There's tremendous variation, just as there is in every other area of sexual activity. Some girls are satisfied with one, while others can't keep themselves from having many. Statistics show that one or two girls out of every ten have more than one orgasm.

A second orgasm usually occurs almost immediately after the first, while the girl is still very much aroused and hasn't come down from her orgasmic peak. But it can also occur after she *does* come down, building up to a new peak twenty or thirty minutes later. For some girls these multiple orgasms may peak ten, thirty, or even fifty times in the course of one sex experience. In such a long series the peaks are often smaller, but every one can be just as satisfying as it is to the woman who has only one.

Another myth that needs discarding is that there's any such thing as a "nymphomaniac," or some kind of disease called "nymphomania." There's nothing at all abnormal about having multiple orgasms or about wanting a great deal of sex. Most women could have several orgasms at a time if they really wanted to try. People believe a "nymphomaniac" is a woman who can't be satisfied sexually, who lives in a state of constant sexual excitement and whether she has orgasm or not, wants to have more and more sex.

This notion was invented by males, and no doubt it's an exciting fantasy for them. It doesn't actually exist in real life, however. My definition of a "nymphomaniac" is a woman who has a higher rate of sexual outlet than the person who calls her that. Or, as Kinsey put it so aptly, "A nymphomaniac is someone who has more sex than you do."

In this time of great concern about the drug culture and about breaking smoking habits or recovering from alcoholism, a new and currently fashionable fad has arisen claiming that sex can be addictive, too, and requires treatment. Again, there is no support in the study of human sexual behavior for such a notion. People have more or less sex for a variety of reasons, and there's the widest possible variation among human beings all over the world. "Addiction" is in the same category as "nymphomania."

If a girl's sexual response is high and constant, there's no reason for her to worry that she's a "nymphomaniac" or an "addict." On the contrary, she should be pleased that she *is* so responsive, and she'll find that she's closer to males in her sexual response.

Still another idea that needs rebuttal is the notion that it's highly desirable if both partners in the sex act have orgasm at the same time. If it happens, that's fine, but it's not important. The intercourse will be pleasurable in any case, under ordinary circumstances. If the partners can't wait for each other, then the one who achieves orgasm first helps the one who's late to come to climax. It *is* important, however, for the partner who hasn't had the orgasm to have one. That may require more intercourse or fondling or both until it happens.

In the sex act itself, whether it's fondling or intercourse, it's still necessary for each partner to be self-centered for the time being, enough to achieve orgasm. Paradoxically, that's the very thing that will bring most pleasure to the other partner.

Even if orgasm *isn't* achieved, it's not the end of the world, as some people think. Either partner can get a great deal of pleasure out of sex simply from the pleasure mutually given. So even though the orgasm is a highly enjoyable experience, it isn't the only good feeling two people can have from sex. There's also the feeling of closeness, the shared pleasure, the blissful intimacy of people who love each other. All these have such definite positive values that the orgasm itself should never be viewed as a tyrant without which the whole act is meaningless.

The girl who's never had an orgasm may be disappointed if she doesn't have one automatically the first time she tries to achieve it by masturbation, fondling, or intercourse. It's something like learning to play tennis, or the piano. You have to learn, through practice, how to build up to this peak. It's easier for some girls than for others. Some take months or years to learn it well. Others achieve it satisfactorily the first time they try. It's a learning process like any other, but a lot more fun.

CHAPTER · 7

The Real Thing

In spite of the fact that most young people don't seem to be worrying about it these days, the argument over whether they should have intercourse before marriage still goes on in many families, even though marriage is no longer necessarily the end result. Conservatives, especially those belonging to fundamentalist religious faiths, want a return to the old strict standards, and they enforce them in their own communities. But a much more permissive generation has now grown up, believing that the question isn't *whether* but *when* teenagers should begin this kind of relationship. Both sides might agree that if this is the course taken, it's a good idea to have as much information about it as possible.

What you decide to do about it depends on several

different factors—parental influence, religious beliefs, personal behavior codes, peer pressure, and purely emotional factors. No one will dispute that having intercourse marks an important change in a young girl's life; consequently she would be wise to know something about what she's doing. That kind of knowledge is the substance of this chapter.

My feeling is that the question isn't nearly as important as it's made out to be. Whether a penis enters a vagina isn't nearly as important as what sort of relationship the two people involved are able to develop, including the kind of sexual adjustment they can make.

When people talk about "premarital sex" or "sex relations" or "sleeping with" someone, they usually mean premarital intercourse.

There's a difference in attitudes between boys and girls about intercourse itself and what it means. To many boys it's a conquest. They've accomplished something, imposed their desires on a girl, and that gives them a feeling of great satisfaction. Most girls, however, don't have any such feelings. Instead they think of intercourse as giving in, accepting, or permitting the male to become victorious. Not many at any early age are prepared to accept the belief that the sexes are equal in this respect. That happens later, if it ever does.

We've come a long way, though, since those earlier times when these differences between males and females were so sharp that a girl was expected to lie down and take whatever the male chose to give her.

Now, if she chooses, a girl can be an equal partner in intercourse—enjoying it, taking part in it actively, being aggressive about it if she feels like it. But even with the new equality, it's still true that intercourse has a somewhat different meaning for a girl. Maybe it's because of the psychological feelings arising from the fact that she's the one being penetrated and the male is doing the penetrating.

If a girl thinks she's going to have to make up her mind about whether to have intercourse, she needs to consider the pros and cons carefully—unless, of course, the decision is made in a moment of arousal when she can't think at all. It's better to consider such an important matter calmly before emotion pushes her into a quick decision she would have been better prepared to make if she'd only thought about the alternatives.

Here are some reasons why a girl might decide to have intercourse for the first time:

1. It may be hard for some people to believe, but the chief reason for having intercourse (aside from the desire to have a baby) is that it's one of the most delightful, exciting, and stimulating experiences a human being can know. It's as natural to want to have intercourse as it is to play tennis, swim, dance, ride a horse, or do anything else that gives pleasure.

It isn't as simple and straightforward as all that, however. Much of the pleasure will be lost if intercourse is accompanied by strong guilt feelings. Girls should also be careful of glorifying intercourse before they've had it. Everything they see on the big and little screens, everything they read about sex, or hear in rock lyrics, leads girls to believe intercourse is the last word in human satisfaction, something almost indescribable. When they get around to having it, they're often disappointed that the world doesn't necessarily stop. Having had some kind of vague anticipation involving much more than the experience is likely to give, a girl may be quite disillusioned and inquire, "Is this all there is to it? Is this what all the shouting is about?" For such girls it may seem to be no more than the kind of feeling they get when they masturbate, heightened only by the presence of a partner.

Girls with more reasonable expectations are likely to find intercourse enjoyable. They haven't been misled by what they see and hear or by parents who have lectured them on the perils of premarital intercourse and so have given them the idea that intercourse must be incredibly wonderful if it's so forbidden. Since this act is an important and permanent part of most people's lives, it's a good idea to get it into perspective from the beginning.

2. For those planning to marry eventually, early intercourse can be a training ground. Valuable lessons can be learned by getting a taste of what it's like to live with someone else in what George Bernard Shaw called "the dreadful intimacy of marriage." That is, the lessons can be valuable if intercourse is performed with good techniques, if it's meaningful to the people involved, if it's part of a whole relationship, and if it's done without feelings of guilt and fear. What is done badly may carry over into marriage or some other relationship. It's like having learned to play tennis from an inadequate instructor and then discovering when you face someone in your first real match that you don't have the strokes you need.

3. Another reason for intercourse is that unlike masturbation, it means interaction with another human being; consequently it's a matter of learning how to live with people—something everyone has to do. It's important, consequently, that intercourse be a giving-and-receiving act.

After marriage, many girls regret that they didn't have premarital intercourse because they now realize what a long, slow learning process it can be. Too late, they and their husbands sometimes discover they're not suited to each other sexually.

As many as 80 percent of girls say the reason they didn't have more intercourse before marriage was because of strong moral objections that prevented them. Another 9 percent have only slight moral objections that stand in the way. Nearly half admit they didn't have more because they were just not interested, while 45 percent are afraid of getting pregnant and the same percentage are afraid of other people's opinion. Fear of AIDS is a strong deterrent today.

4. If early intercourse is with a boy a girl expects to marry or live with, it's a good way for her to find out if she's going to enjoy the constant intimacy of the bedroom with that particular young man, and of course it gives him the same opportunity. Whatever kind of relationship she expects to establish, she'll discover quickly whether she and her partner are completely suited to each other. Sometimes people are suited in every way *except* sexually. People who discover this after marriage often divorce, or else have to seek help from a therapist. First times have to be a fair test, however. Intercourse has to take place in the most relaxed atmosphere. If it's done with strong guilt feelings, or done furtively and hastily, it isn't like marriage or any other kind of lasting relationship, so it's not a fair test.

5. People learn more easily when they're young. If learning is correct from the beginning, sexual adjustment in marriage is much easier.

6. Some girls rush into intercourse because their friends are having it and they think they'll lose status in the group if they don't. That's powerful pressure, but it's the worst reason for beginning intercourse.

So much for the reasons. What else should be considered?

1. First, and most obvious, the danger of pregnancy. That isn't as serious a problem as it used to be because most girls have access to some kind of contraceptive. This doesn't mean everything has become perfectly safe, as we thought when the pill was first introduced. Some girls and women have undesirable side effects from it, and recently the specter of cancer, with continued use over a long period of time, has been raised. Some doctors refuse to prescribe it because of this and other long-range possible effects on health. There are, of course, other kinds of contraception, and we'll be talking about these methods shortly. One thing that can be said for all of them is that if a proper contraceptive is available and is used properly, the possibility of pregnancy is virtually eliminated.

2. Sexually transmitted disease, including AIDS, is another danger, and I'll talk about this subject later. For now, here's a preliminary red flag: We don't have quite the freedom from danger we thought we had when modern drugs like penicillin were introduced, much less a cure for AIDS.

3. A common danger is pregnancy that results in a forced marriage—not a good way to enter the married state. The boy and girl might have married each other in any case, but more often than not, one of them has a more difficult time making the marriage work if she (or he) has been forced into it. The rate of failure in these marriages is high.

4. Heavy guilt is another negative factor. If it exists, there's likely to be damage of some kind. I believe this is the most important reason for not having early intercourse. Guilt is determined by the attitude each person brings to the act, and it's better not to have intercourse at all if either person feels extremely guilty and is likely to suffer attacks of conscience afterward.

5. Some girls fear a boy will lose respect for them if they have intercourse with him, and no doubt that can happen. But more often it's not so much a loss of respect as it is the boy's simply chalking up another conquest and moving on to the next girl, to the hurt and bewilderment of the first one. It's hard to do, I know, but a girl should make some honest effort to decide whether a boy is more concerned about her as an individual, a whole person, than he is with one particular part of her body—the vagina.

6. Fear about what may happen if you're caught may prove to be another source of guilt later on. The worst that can happen is public knowledge and disapproval from school, parents, clergy, police, relatives, even friends. People don't usually get caught, however, and if they are, how they feel about it depends a great deal on who catches them. What really complicates matters is being found out by disapproving parents. If it's a friend or someone your own age, nothing much more than embarrassment results.

Responsible girls (and boys) who have thought about the pros and cons and then decided to have intercourse will have to accept the risks that may be involved. It will help if they think about their high school driving classes. There they learn to drive defensively. In thinking about intercourse, they should minimize the risks in the same way.

7. A very real danger is the possibility that the physical side of a relationship may become the most important part of it. If that's the case, a girl would be better off not to have it. As I've said earlier, the value of early intercourse is that it should become an important part of a *whole* relationship between people, not just an isolated experience. If a girl thinks a boy only wants to have sex with her, and still goes ahead with intercourse, she may wind up with a sexual partner who isn't necessarily a friend.

8. Even though you may or may not agree, it can't be overlooked that many people think intercourse without marriage is morally wrong. More girls than boys believe this, obviously. For the growing numbers of those who belong to fundamentalist faiths (and that includes a large number of young people), their view is an essential part of their religion.

The double standard has always prevailed until recently; people think premarital sex is wrong for girls, but they wink at what boys do. That attitude hasn't disappeared, by any means, even in the so-called New Age. But equality of the sexes should mean equal responsibility, in sexual as well as in other areas of living. If premarital sex is morally wrong for a girl, it should be just as wrong for a boy.

The problem of early sex, whether it's premarital or just early, comes down to a question of how a girl feels about it, whether she thinks it's right or wrong. If she thinks it's wrong, none of the reasons I've listed for having it will make any difference to her. Similarly, if she thinks it's *not* wrong, she will certainly do it, and the only problems that remain are time, place, and partner. Before she jumps into something irrevocable, however, she should do a little careful thinking for her own protection. Will that happen? Not if a girl is carried away by the moment, by the powerful sex impulse that blots out any consideration of rights or wrongs, or any thought of what a boy's attitudes about it may be. The time to think responsibly comes *before* that moment.

Today it's not so much a question of *whether* inter course is going to happen early, but *when*, and that's an important question, too. As I've said, the best time to begin intercourse is when a girl feels she's ready for it and can handle all its implications. Some reach this stage very early, some later. It makes no sense to set an arbitrary age.

But let's assume the decision has been made, and you intend to have intercourse. Like so many other girls, you may not know exactly what to expect or even what to do. In that case the experience is likely to be a fumbling and unsatisfactory one. For instance, if you've never seen an erect male penis, it may frighten you to think of such a large object penetrating you and you may even wonder if it's possible. But as I noted earlier in describing the female's sexual anat omy, what seems like a mere slit at the opening of the vagina is actually an opening of amazing flexibility. Remembering that a baby is born through that same opening should dispose of any fear that the stretching by a penis might be painful. When you're aroused there's an additional help in the lubrication of the vagina by secretions from the glands. That makes in sertion of the penis very easy. Sex play before inser tion causes these secretions.

When it comes down to actual intercourse, the traditional position in our culture (sometimes called "the missionary position") is for the girl to lie on her back with her legs apart, while the boy lies on her, face to face, with his legs together. Nearly every girl under stands that much. She can help the boy insert his pe his, but more often he does it by himself, gradually, making small thrusts forward.

If you're a virgin, the hymen will be broken by this penetration, with a quick twinge of pain that's over almost immediately. Sometimes, though, the hymen may be tougher and the boy has to push with more force to break it. In that case there may be a little more pain and discomfort, and a girl may not enjoy her first intercourse for that reason. Satisfaction will come later. If a girl is unprepared for this possibility, she may find sex distasteful, and take a long time to get over the unpleasantness of her first experience.

But as I noted in Chapter 2, many girls have their hymens broken before they ever have intercourse. It can happen through exercise, sports, or masturbation. Any psychological problems involved in this first attempt can be minimized if a boy fondles a girl a great deal and inserts his fingers in her vagina before he puts in his penis. Once it's penetrated, the vagina clasps the penis in a velvet grip and intercourse continues with a series of pelvic thrusts, increasing in speed, frequency, and force as excitement mounts and the act moves toward orgasm.

A common problem is for the male to ejaculate too quickly, before a girl has her own orgasm. He can prevent this from happening if he understands the problem, but since this is not often the case, a girl can help by slowing him down, insisting on more fondling before he inserts his penis so that she'll be nearer orgasm herself.

This slowing-down process can also be helped by

using different positions, which also provide variet
for couples having regular intercourse. One of th
best positions to accomplish this is for the girl to lie o
top of the boy, with her legs together between his, o
vice versa. She can help him and herself by then hav
ing him put his hands on her buttocks, pushing he
pelvic area toward his and making it easier for her t
thrust and build up tension for orgasm. The weight o
her body also reduces movement, and that also help
delay ejaculation. A variation of this position, on
more commonly used, is for the girl to sit astride th
boy, with penis inserted, riding him at her own pace
She then controls the speed of the intercourse hersel
and while the boy will probably move beneath her, a
she would beneath him, he isn't likely to have orgasm
quite as soon and she can prolong things as sh
pleases.

In still another position, the girl and boy lie o
their sides facing each other, with the girl's leg thrown
over the boy's, permitting them to get closer together
This position can also be reversed, with the boy lying
on his side *behind* the girl, inserting his penis in he
vagina and using his free hand to stimulate her clitori
or breasts. There's also the position people call "dog
gie fashion," in which the girl kneels instead of lying
on her side, and again the boy inserts his penis from
behind. Or she can lie on her stomach, with the bo
lying on her, or on her back with the boy beneath her
again leaving him free to stimulate her with his hand
In fact, in the search for variety, people can have inter

course standing up or sitting down. Human ingenuity has few limits.

If a girl thinks some of these positions are "weird," she should know that they exist around the world, in even more variety than I've described. In one of the South Sea Islands, for example, the man kneels or squats in front of the woman, who is lying on her back with her legs spread and rises just enough to permit insertion. In short, there are so many ways to have intercourse that there isn't any "right" or "wrong" way. "Right" is what works best for the people involved. What may seem strange to one couple is commonplace for another. There's no such thing as a "normal" position, and if the one in which a woman lies on her back is the most common one, that doesn't mean it's any more "normal."

When intercourse is over, there's another difference between males and females. A male usually feels let down immediately. He wants to withdraw and go to sleep or otherwise detach himself from the female. But she may want more penetration, or at least more love play, and she appreciates the man (or boy) who understands this, thinks of her need, and does something about it. A girl who knows about this difference herself can explain it to a boy.

If a girl or a boy wants to get out of bed immediately and wash or take a shower, that may reflect an attitude about sex built in since childhood—the feeling that sex is something dirty. Sometimes a girl isn't happy about the act itself, but she should never feel that there's anything unclean about the secretions from either her body or his.

Since love, or at least affection, is the motivation for most girls to have intercourse, it's no wonder they're curious about those who do it for money. Young girls often look upon prostitutes with mingled fascination and disgust. They find it hard to understand how a woman could have intercourse with just *any* man, and for money at that. In prostitution—"the life," as prostitutes call it—there is seldom any affection, friendship, or interchange of feelings. There may even be hostility involved in these encounters, especially on the part of the man. The whole thing is a depressing experience for some men. For a prostitute the act may be an expression of continuing hatred for the male sex, but on the other hand, contrary to popular belief, some prostitutes may actually enjoy sex with many different men and have orgasm with some of them.

But the contrast is striking. In prostitution the act is usually performed in a drab room somewhere, a rooming house or a fourth-class hotel, and this sordid setting reflects the nature of the act. But the same lack of emotional content may exist if the prostitute is paid hundreds of dollars and the act is performed in an expensive hotel or apartment. What's important is the fact that even if intercourse takes place between people who have only warm feelings for each other, the quality of the act may be affected by the setting. I'm emphasizing that aspect of it because it also has a bearing on the possibility of interruption, which is much more important for a girl than a boy.

If a girl decides to have intercourse, she should be choosy about where she has it. The first requirement is that it be a place where the possibility of discovery is at a minimum. The almost traditional place—a car beside the road or in a "lover's lane"—is common, but it's usually so cramped and uncomfortable that it's a poor place to have a first experience. It's also becoming more and more dangerous as crimes like rape and robbery begin to reach beyond the usual places. Some people with psychological problems get sexual pleasure out of creeping up on parked cars and looking inside, but these same problems make them unpredictable.

Probably the next most common place is the house of either the boy or the girl. That's a good idea only if they can be absolutely sure that the parents won't return home unexpectedly. If there's any doubt about it, anxiety and tension will almost inevitably surround the act. Motel and hotel rooms are a third option, but they're not always accessible to younger couples. Places like the woods, a beach, or some really secluded area are the best bets for the uninterrupted privacy that insures peaceful enjoyment of the act.

I hope no girl who reads this will think I'm minimizing the importance of the step a girl takes when she decides to have intercourse for the first time. It's a major step that can't be retracted. It may be true that a large part of society makes too much of it, but we have to remember that it *is*, for several reasons, one of the most important actions in a girl's life. For one thing, once she's had intercourse, she'll never be a virgin again, whether the hymen is broken or not and regardless of whether it means anything to her. Virginity is more a state of mind than it is a condition of the body.

I'm thinking now of a fifteen-year-old girl—warm, open, affectionate, who hasn't developed any guilt feelings about sex. In the course of a long relationship with a boyfriend, there's been a steadily increasing emotional development with each other. Along with that, there's been intense and protracted fondling, but without intercourse. Inevitably, in such a relationship, intercourse is going to occur at some point.

In her mind, this girl hasn't made any sudden or dramatic change in her virgin status. Having intercourse has been only another expression of her deep fondness for the boy. Probably she thinks she loves him, and it may be she does. But if the relationship is broken off later, and she begins a new relationship with another boy, she won't enter into it, as a result of her previous behavior, with any different feelings toward herself than those she had in her earlier relationship.

While intercourse isn't the big deal it's often made out to be, it *does* provide a certain completeness in a relationship. If people feel open and loving toward each other, they may still erect certain barriers between them by mutual consent—no fondling below the waist, for instance, or doing everything *but* having intercourse. A certain restraint is bound to develop in those circumstances. I'm not suggesting that barriers should be tossed aside. I'm only saying it's better to face those barriers consciously, understanding the pros and cons of erecting them. In sex, as in every other aspect of human relationships, understanding is the glue that holds everything together.

CHAPTER · 8

Consequences of the Real Thing

Pregnancy is the most obvious consequence of intercourse. It's not quite the problem it once was because of the greatly increased access to contraceptives girls have today, but the statistics tell us that teen-age pregnancies are still a major concern for girls. Some can't afford contraceptives, others use them carelessly or not at all, and in any case, none of these devices is 100 percent safe.

Abortion is an option if pregnancy occurs, but it has become one of the most controversial issues in American life, with fierce opinions on both sides and much else involved besides the fact of the abortion itself. Until the famous *Roe v. Wade* decision by the

United States Supreme Court, which permitted it with qualifications, abortion was not legal under any circumstances. It occurred anyway, of course, with the operation very often performed by unqualified doctors under squalid circumstances. Until recently an abortion has been relatively easy to obtain, and it is performed by thoroughly qualified doctors under the best conditions.

But the abortion situation was confused in 1989 by a new Supreme Court ruling on the subject. Under the 1973 *Roe v. Wade* decision, the states were forbidden to interfere during the first three months of pregnancy. Abortion, it said, was a matter between a woman and her doctor during that time, but some restrictions were placed on the second three months, and during the last three, the states were permitted to regulate. In its new ruling, *Webster v. Reproductive Health Services*, a Missouri law was upheld sharply restricting abortion services and requiring doctors to test for the viability of a fetus at twenty weeks. Whether there will be further restrictions as the result of pending cases, in effect possibly overturning *Roe v. Wade* and making abortion illegal once more, remains to be seen.

In spite of everything, however, the number of teen-age pregnancies remains a social problem. It disturbs or destroys careers and life prospects, and it's a problem not easily solved. Moralists argue that it can be avoided simply by forbidding girls to have intercourse—"just say no," as they're advised to do with drugs—but no one familiar with everyday teen-age life takes this argument seriously.

It's easy enough for people to condemn the pregnant teen-ager, and some do, but it's a far more constructive thing to help her. Some school systems, especially in urban areas where the pregnancy rate is high, set up classes especially for these girls so that they can continue their schooling while they get instruction in parental and maternal care. The results are generally excellent.

For obvious reasons, however, it's better to prevent pregnancy if possible. Since mankind's earliest days, attempts have been made to avoid it by using some kind of contraceptive device, although the usefulness and practicality of such devices where young girls are concerned are not always satisfactory. Every contraceptive device has some controversy surrounding it. Let's consider them one by one.

Withdrawal is probably the one most commonly used by young people, if they don't have the money, opportunity, or motivation to use mechanical devices. It sounds simple and easy—to withdraw before ejaculation and avoid having to use any apparatus, but like so many other things, it isn't that easy and simple.

A comparatively minor drawback is that it diminishes enjoyment. At the height of sexual excitement, when both people are most involved and the boy wants to keep on pushing in, he feels himself coming to orgasm and hastily pulls out. There's always the possibility he'll be so excited he doesn't remember to do it. But even if he does, there may be enough sperm in the lubricating fluid coming out of his penis before he ejaculates to make a girl pregnant. It's also possible for a boy to ejaculate at the opening of the vagina, and even though the girl may still have her hymen intact, sperm can find their way through and move all the way up the length of the vagina into the uterus. So withdrawal is unsatisfactory at best, and in the bargain it's unsafe. No wonder we have the old saying that the biggest lie a boy can tell a girl is "Don't worry, I won't get you pregnant. I won't come inside you."

Another highly impractical method is to avoid having intercourse when the egg is in the process of coming out of the ovary and down into the Fallopian tubes. That would work if we could be absolutely sure when it's happening. We know that pregnancy can be avoided by not having intercourse during the few hours of the month when this process occurs. The problem is how to be sure. If a girl kept an accurate record of her menstrual periods, it would be possible to pinpoint the process at fourteen days before she began the next menstruation. But such a record would be useful only if she had regular periods, which many girls don't, and if she ovulated only once a month. Some girls ovulate more often.

A good many people attempt to use this method because it's the only one approved by the Catholic Church. But this "rhythm method," as it's called, is so uncertain that it can't be recommended if a couple doesn't want a baby. If they don't really care whether they have one or not, it can be regarded as a somewhat half-hearted method of contraception. It's often unsuccessful.

Perhaps the most effective means of contraception

is the rubber sheath called the condom, which fits over the penis, contains the semen, and prevents the sperm from going into the uterus. The method is centuries old. Before rubber was invented, silk handkerchiefs or other fabrics were used. Condoms (also commonly knows as "safeties" and "rubbers") can be bought at drugstores, or from vending machines at filling stations and elsewhere. They have become even more prevalent since the AIDS epidemic began. Relatively cheap, they're used only once. Breakage rarely occurs, nor do pinholes that might permit semen to ooze through. Federal law requires only every tenth one to be inspected, but companies that make them inspect each one.

Even so, it's wise to take some simple precautions. For example, it's a bad idea to carry condoms around for a long time without using them—say three months or more—especially if the package is open to the air. Rubber deteriorates. You'd better be sure the boy you may be planning to have intercourse with knows that. Now that some girls carry condoms with them and insist on a boy's wearing one to avoid both AIDS and pregnancy, *both* partners can take precautionary measures.

A girl should also know that occasionally a condom will slip off the penis during intercourse. If it does— stop! She should also be sure that the boy holds the end of the condom before withdrawing, so that no semen is spilled, and that he withdraws his penis immediately after he has orgasm; otherwise, his erection will diminish and the condom will either come off inside or let semen escape. Condoms aren't 100 percent safe, but they're about 99 percent effective. They are the best contraceptive available, possibly excepting the pill, which we'll talk about later.

Substitutes for condoms should never be used, even if a friend recommends one. Some boys make crude and ineffective attempts to manufacture them out of rubber balloons, or even substances like plastic wrap. These devices are little better than no protection at all.

Another method of contraception is for the girl to wash out her vagina after intercourse with water containing an antiseptic. This is known as a douche (pronounced *doosh*). It requires a douche bag, an apparatus that looks like a hot-water bottle with a tube. It forces water into the vagina. Since it's so unwieldy, girls aren't likely to carry one around, and that fact has led to some unusual substitutes. One is to take a cola bottle, shake it up, and squirt it into the vagina by placing the thumb partly over the top. But any such technique, and especially this one, is an extremely poor and ineffective method of contraception. A large number of pregnancies have resulted from it. If antiseptics are used, some of them can burn or irritate the vagina.

Still another contraceptive method, used much more by married women than young girls, at least until recently, is a dome-shaped vaginal cap made of rubber. It must be fitted by a doctor, since it comes in different sizes to accommodate various sizes of women. This cap is called a diaphragm, and it fits over the cervix, closing off the entrance to the uterus so the sperm can't enter. A doctor fits it to be sure the size is right, but then a girl (or woman) has to learn to put it in herself before intercourse. She must use a special cream or jelly with it and has to leave it in for eight hours afterward.

Few young girls have used this device until recently because doctors were unwilling to fit unmarried girls without parental consent. Not many physicians make such moral judgments these days unless they have strong religious convictions. Some still require parental consent, but if a girl has a good relationship with her doctor, she'll have no problems. If she doesn't, she can always change doctors.

Some women don't use the diaphragm but insert foams, creams, jellies, suppositories, or tablets (all available at drugstores) into their vaginas. None of these is as safe as a condom, and in any case most girls don't like to use them because they think these remedies are too messy.

A revolution in contraception came with the introduction several years ago of the oral contraceptive popularly known as "the pill." This is how it works. A girl takes these pills, one a day, for twenty-one days and then stops in order to menstruate. The pills are being refined and improved constantly, but they still have possible side effects. Some girls feel sick or put on weight. A doctor has to prescribe these pills and then watch his patient for a few months to see what the effects are and whether she's affected more by one kind than by another.

Recently doctors have raised more serious questions about the pill, and some refuse to prescribe them. But side effects are relatively uncommon, and it appears to depend on the girl. Some react, some don't, just as they would to other kinds of medication. Nothing has been firmly established about the pill's long-range effects, including its possible carcinogenic effects. But any girl who fears taking it for any reason shouldn't do it. The anxiety about intercourse wouldn't be worth it. At the moment, however, the pill is the best method of contraception we have until something better comes along.

Use of the pill has leveled off somewhat, but in any case very few young girls will be likely to use it, for obvious reasons. For the older ones who do, it can be said that this method, if it's properly used, ends fear of pregnancy. If it fails, it's usually because of human error, especially carelessness about taking the pills.

There is also the intrauterine device commonly known as the IUD. It's made of plastic, comes in several different shapes, and has to be inserted into the uterus by a doctor and left there for months, even years. For a time it appeared to be an ideal method because it was easily inserted and was virtually guaranteed to prevent pregnancy. There was a major drawback, however. Not every woman who hadn't had a child could use it. Then, recently, serious questions have been raised about its safety. Girls who have multiple sexual partners and use an IUD may develop pelvic inflammation. Other dangerous possibilities, not yet established, have been raised. Consequently there is less enthusiasm for the device these days, although some doctors continue to prescribe it.

Contraception can be the responsibility of either the male or female. Males continue to use withdrawal and the condom as their chief techniques until a "pill" is developed for them, something that may not be far off after considerable experimentation. All the others are methods females use, and as I said earlier, many girls and women have taken on the condom too. For teen-agers the condom is still the best available device. It places considerable responsibility in the hands of the boy. A girl might supply him with one, but he has to use it properly.

A completely different aspect of the problem is that girls, in general, have a more romantic concept of sex and intercourse than boys. Many of them don't consciously intend to have intercourse but get carried away by the moment and the situation and have it without any thought of contraception. Any planning or thought about whether a boy has a condom on before intercourse goes up in the smoke of sexual excitement. For most girls, in any case, planning ahead takes away from the pleasure of intercourse. They want it to be spontaneous and not interrupted mechanically.

That's another reason girls don't like using the various foams, jellies, and suppositories available, even though they don't require a doctor's prescription, are easy to use, and are relatively inexpensive. A girl may be dismayed, for example, if the little almond-shaped suppositories don't melt when they should, or don't melt completely. Or they melt too easily and girls think it's messy to insert them, even if they know these suppositories *must* melt because it's the chemicals they contain that coat the vagina and kill the sperm. Cream does the same job when it's used with the diaphragm. The rubber cap only holds the cream in place against the opening of the uterus.

Since all these devices have to be inserted into the vagina just before intercourse, girls are inclined to think they don't want to interrupt the rhythm of their lovemaking and pause to do something so unromantic. The cream may also leak out the next day as a discharge. Foams, however, disappear during intercourse and have no odor. Still, they have to be used with an applicator. Girls who insert the foam several hours before they think they're going to have intercourse are taking a chance. The interval should be no longer than an hour.

I understand how girls feel about these mechanical and possibly "messy" devices, but at the same time I have to say that the surest way to get pregnant is to be overcome by excitement, disregard what may happen, and refuse to do anything about the possible consequences. We have so many teen-age pregnancies not because the contraceptive devices fail but because they're used either improperly or not at all.

Let's assume now, however, that a girl *does* become pregnant. The first indication, as most girls know, is when a period is missed. Pregnancy can then be confirmed by testing. Now there are four options open to her. She can get married, but that's usually not a real choice because both the boy and girl are likely to be too young to start family life. Nor can they simply start living together, as they might if they were older. Few boys are able to support a girl at that age, and it means schooling will probably be interrupted or even ended for both of them. And as I've said, marriages begun under these circumstances are usually not as successful as those made without pressure.

A second option is to have the baby without marrying the boy. But that may not be a good choice either, because the girl usually isn't able to support a baby herself and give it the right environment to grow up in. If she has to quit school, go to work, and rely on her mother and day-care centers to take the child during working hours, she's still likely to have a great many emotional and economic problems.

The third option is to have the baby but permit it to be adopted immediately. Numerous complications can occur if this is the road taken. If she wants to keep her pregnancy secret, a girl will have to arrange somehow to leave her community for five or six months. When she has the baby, after going through the nine months of pregnancy, she may not want to give it up. That often happens, no matter how sensible it might be to carry out the adoption. Putting up a baby for adoption is an emotional, painful process for most girls.

Then, finally, there's abortion. Besides whatever legal complications there may be (if any), there are other complications. If a girl is religious, or comes from a religious family, especially if she's a Catholic, she has an immediate problem. Catholics believe as a matter of doctrine that the soul enters the fetus at the moment of conception, and so they oppose abortion, as do other "right-to-life" advocates, who consider abortion the same as murder. Most physicians disagree, arguing that life doesn't really begin until the time, during the last three months, when a baby can live outside the womb.

Millions of women do have abortions these days. They are relatively easy to obtain from qualified doctors and are performed under the best conditions, as I've said. Done properly, they're safer than a tonsillectomy. It can be dangerous only in the hands of incompetent doctors or abortionists who aren't even doctors and work under unsterile conditions.

If a girl thinks she's pregnant, the first thing she should do is to make certain. That's done by means of a medical test, using either a blood or urine sample. It's relatively inexpensive and can be obtained from a doctor. Do-it-yourself tests are available over the counter at the drugstore, but they are probably less reliable than a laboratory's report to a doctor.

Once pregnancy is established, the best advice is to do what most girls, I'm sure, dread most. Nevertheless it's her parents she should turn to first for help. True, many parents will give their daughter a rough time and perhaps even treat her shabbily if she's pregnant without being married. On the other hand, there are many who turn out to be warm, loving, and protective in this situation. Naturally, they'll probably blame the boy and be angry with him, even though they may be unfair in doing so, but that's a common reaction.

Sometimes a girl can turn to other adults in the community—her doctor, a clergyman, or more likely, an adult in the family to whom she feels especially close, possibly an aunt or uncle, or an older married sister.

If abortion is to be the option, remember that it must be done before the end of the third month, because after that the fetus becomes progressively larger and makes the operation more difficult. Often, perhaps in most cases, doctors won't perform an abortion after the third month.

One thing to be avoided absolutely is reliance on a self-administered drug or some other means of bringing on a miscarriage, in which the fetus is loosened from the uterine walls and slips down the vagina and out of the body. Drugs that are popularly believed to cause miscarriage—quinine, castor oil, ergot, among others—almost never do. If they ever work, it's only because the girl would have had the miscarriage in any case. About one in eight pregnancies ends in miscarriage in the ordinary course of events.

If a girl is afraid she might have become pregnant, she can get pills or an injection from her doctor if she sees him no later than the next day after intercourse. Such medication is often effective in preventing pregnancy.

It's worse trying to induce abortion by some such means as falling on the stomach, inserting something into the uterus, or jumping from a chair or table to jar the fetus loose. These are extremely dangerous practices, often leading to injury, infection, or death. Even if they were likely to work, the danger would be far too great.

Pregnancy isn't the only consequence of intercourse, however. Sexually transmitted diseases occur through some sort of sexual contact, and that danger is present, too. AIDS is at the top of the list these days because, unlike the others, it is almost always fatal and, as of 1990, there was no known cure. Until this virus appeared, the two most common sexually transmitted diseases for centuries were syphilis and gonorrhea. Since they're more common, let's talk about them first.

In gonorrhea the symptoms are largely the same for girls as for boys. But because the girl's sex organs are more hidden, her symptoms will be more difficult to spot. A boy will notice a burning in his penis when he urinates, a symptom appearing eight to fifteen days after he's infected. A little later, pus with a characteristic and rather unpleasant odor begins to drip from the penis. Girls, however, have a painful infection in the lining of the urethra, which also produces pus. But since the secretion is not so easily noticed as it is in boys, she may think she has nothing more than a vaginal infection.

Syphilis is a more serious matter. The germ invades the body through any mucous membrane. In a girl, that can be the vagina or the mouth. The first symptom is a single sore, which is not painful. This is followed by a rash, appearing on any part of the body.

It's a light rash, lasting for only a short time, and so it may go unnoticed. The sore appears most often on the penis of the boy or the vaginal lips of the girl, about sixty days after the infection. It goes away in time. If the disease is not treated, however, it continues to fester in the body silently, although it may seem to disappear entirely and not return for months or even years. When it does return, it will be in a much more violent form, able to do serious damage to body organs, and if it's unchecked, may eventually end in death.

A girl develops the same characteristic syphilis sore, or chancre, as the boy, but it may be hidden in the vagina or the mouth so she may not know she has it. Incidentally, there's no truth in the common superstition that you can tell if a girl has venereal disease by pouring whiskey or a carbonated soft drink on her sex organ, and if it burns, she's infected. The only way a girl can tell is by an examination that shows a visible chancre on the lips of her vagina, something she can see for herself, or if she has a discharge of pus from the vagina or urethra, or more commonly, by having a blood test.

These ancient forms of sexually transmitted disease (the early explorers brought them to America) are not the scourge they used to be. Gonorrhea could once be cured only by long and sometimes painful treatment, if it was cured at all. Syphilis ran rampant through the world, unchecked for centuries, ending the lives of millions. Even in modern times, it's been called "the great killer." But the discovery of penicillin and the sulfa drugs has brought both diseases under control.

Like any other controllable diseases, however, individual cases must be identified and treated, particularly now, when resistant strains of the germs have been appearing. That's why it's important not to treat them lightly. Don't listen to anyone who repeats that old cliché "It's no worse than a bad cold." Without treatment the consequences are far worse than a bad cold, and in the case of syphilis, they can be fatal.

A girl who has any symptoms of such a disease, or thinks she has, should consult her doctor at once. Young girls (and boys) are likely to be afraid that a doctor will tell their parents if they do have a disease, but most doctors respect the confidential nature of the relationship between doctor and patient, even if it's a family doctor who may have delivered her. But the doctor *is* required by law to report the case to the local board of health, although not all of them do so. Unquestionably, there are a great many unreported cases.

The board of health is interested in only one thing. It wants to know where the girl or boy got the disease, and it has the authority to ask them the identity of anyone they've had intercourse with, and then to examine these people to find out where the infection originated. This is embarrassing, but it's the best way to lower the disease rate. It should be emphasized that the board of health isn't interested in making moral judgments. It doesn't want to condemn or expose people, only to track down the source of the infection consequently identity is protected.

Penicillin shots are the treatment for both syphilis and gonorrhea. The series lasts about five days for syphilis, one day for gonorrhea, and it's almost always effective. We're fortunate to have such a simple and quick cure for these diseases. If everybody cooperated with the board of health in the way I've described, we would be able to keep STDs (sexually transmitted diseases) under even better control.

There are two other sexually transmitted diseases that are less well known, and you should know about them too. One is called NGU, meaning nongonococcal urethritis. This is now the most prevalent venereal disease and probably the most common one that's sexually transmitted. Until recently it was considered to be only a minor problem, but then it was discovered that it could cause lifelong sterility in men and women if not treated. Some specialists believe that one variety of NGU bacteria is possibly more dangerous than gonococcus. Since most girls and women don't have symptoms indicating the presence of NGU and so become carriers without knowing it, and since cases aren't usually reported to health officials, as gonorrhea and syphilis are, it has spread rapidly until it now affects more than two million people a year. While it doesn't usually respond to penicillin, other antibiotics are effective. You should see your doctor if you notice anything unusual, such as pain or a discharge, in your genital area.

Another sexually transmitted disease not quite as

well known as the others until recently is the result of an invasion by the germs called herpes simplex—the same ones that cause cold sores. They can spread through sexual contact and the result is an extremely painful infection of the genitals in both men and women. It isn't fatal or damaging to organs, but it's enough to put those who have it out of the running for some time, and it's not pleasant to have. No cure is yet available, and unfortunately the disease tends to re-cur.

Overshadowing all the diseases I've been talking about, however, is the great plague of our century, AIDS. You may have been getting some AIDS educa-tion at your school or from some other source—news-papers and magazines have been full of information—but in case you haven't heard or read the facts, here they are.

AIDS means Acquired Immune Deficiency Syn-drome. It's a viral infection that destroys the body's natural immune system. As I've said, there is no known cure and therefore it has to be presumed fatal, sooner or later. As the immune system breaks down, patients are made more vulnerable to all kinds of in-fections, tumors, neurological disorders, and other diseases. Often the breakdown takes the form of a very dangerous lung infection, or a form of skin cancer, or both. The skin cancer once affected mostly elderly men and was slow-acting; it was not sexually transmit-ted. But in AIDS patients it is rapid and devastating. AIDS is a worldwide disease, possibly originating in

Africa, where there are great numbers of cases in both men and women.

Scientists and researchers are still learning about AIDS. Some believe that being infected by HIV (immuno-deficiency virus) is not enough in itself to cause AIDS, and that other factors have to be present— another virus, perhaps, or a previous weakening of the immune system.

Numerous other questions await answers. It isn't clear, for example, how many of those infected with the virus will actually develop AIDS, and if they do, when it will happen. It's likely, not certain, that they'll be infectious to others throughout their lives, even if they never develop the disease. It may also be true that some develop light or severe symptoms after an amount of time that no one can pinpoint, but they may never actually have what can be unmistakably identified as AIDS. Even these "milder" cases can lead to death. No statistics are available, but there may be as many as ten times the number of such cases as those who have AIDS, and the number of infected people with no symptoms at all is a hundred times higher than those with the "mild" cases.

It's incorrect to say that you "catch" AIDS. You may be infected by the virus, and you may or may not wind up having AIDS over a period of time. You can get the virus only by very intimate physical contact. The virus has been isolated in the blood, semen, vaginal secretions, mother's milk, saliva, urine, feces, even tears. Most experts agree, however, that transmission is possible only through the exchange of blood, semen, or vaginal secretions because the concentration of the virus in the other sources would require exchanging an inordinate amount of fluid. Many authorities believe there are factors in saliva that kill HIV.

Consequently AIDS infection can be acquired through blood transfusions, through the sharing of unsterilized needles among drug users, or if infected blood from an open wound comes into contact with an abrasion, break, or cut in another person's skin. Most of the time, however, infection occurs during intimate sexual contact, when several of these fluids pass from one body to another. Infected semen, for example, may enter the body through oral, vaginal, or anal intercourse.

In our anxiety about the spread of AIDS we're inclined to forget that it's not transmitted all that easily and that it can't be transmitted through casual contact. The virus can't be sent through the air; you can't get it by shaking hands with an infected person or even by hugging and dry kissing. Nor can you get it by sharing a workplace or a schoolroom or a household with an infected person. Of course, it would be dangerous to share such things as toothbrushes or razor blades.

There are five major groups at risk: homosexual and bisexual men, the latter far more numerous than the former; intravenous-drug users who share needles; sexual partners of people in these two groups; their sexual partners; and children conceived, born, and nursed by infected mothers.

Does that mean we have to stop having sex? Not at

all. But if you have sexual contact with someone, you should assume, for the sake of safety and to protect your life, that the other person may be carrying the AIDS virus, even though he may have no idea that he does. This means you should avoid any risky behavior and take the precautions I've discussed earlier to avoid both disease and pregnancy. You should do this even though it's true that most people are not at risk. Anything that prevents the exchange of fluids is the front line of defense, and using spermicides will make things even safer. If they're sexually active, both boys and girls should carry condoms, lubricated with non-oxynol-9 (which can kill the AIDS virus), and know how to use them. Boys can be infected by boys *and* girls; using condoms protects both sexes.

Here's a prime rule: Never have sex when you're drunk or high. That's the time you don't take precautions, and it could be your last chance to take them. Anyway, sex is its own high. Drug users should never share intravenous needles, and no one should have unprotected sex with anyone who has ever shared those needles. No matter how much you want to have sex, and how urgent the opportunity may be, remember that none of this is worth risking unprotected intercourse. Dying from AIDS is one of the worst ways to go. And don't let yourself be talked into sex for non-sexual reasons. Don't depend on the other person to provide protection or the good judgment required in sexual situations. Don't give in to being begged or threatened.

You should also consider that satisfactory sex is

possible without penetrating the vagina, thus avoiding the possibility of either AIDS or pregnancy. A couple may caress and stroke each other, followed by masturbating the other person while he, or she, does it to you. In this case, however, to be absolutely safe, nonoxynol-9 should be applied to the fingers beforehand, and the hands washed afterward. It can also be satisfying if both you and your partner masturbate yourselves while lying together and caressing each other. That, of course, would be safer than any other method. While you're avoiding AIDS and pregnancy, you can also be discovering things about your personal sexuality you didn't know before.

I hope all these warnings won't frighten girls (or boys, either) into a life of celibacy. That isn't very likely, I know. It's simply a matter of recognizing a great danger and being sensible about it. People have a right to sex, but they also have a responsibility, and never more so than in the case of AIDS.

Whatever the consequences of intercourse may be —and I've covered the most important ones, I think— the best advice I can give any girl is to learn about these consequences before she makes any decisions about whether to have intercourse. If she has that knowledge beforehand, she'll not only be far better able to make a decision, but the consequences, if they occur, won't be unexpected.

Beyond that, the most difficult consequences of

intercourse for most girls to handle are the feelings of fear or guilt, or both, that the act may create. Since these factors are the enemy of any meaningful human relationship, a girl who finds she can't handle these feelings would be better off not to have intercourse at all, and thus avoid the struggle over consequences entirely.

But even if there's no fear or guilt, and even if a girl has weighed her decision carefully before taking so important a step (unfortunately, these conditions aren't very common), intercourse may produce unforeseen psychological consequences. A girl may feel that she's not ready for such an intimate relationship after all, or that she's created a situation that disturbs and upsets her way of life. Sometimes, in a moment of regret, she may feel that she's given herself away too easily—for no more than a quick sensation. It's not uncommon, too, for her to see her partner in a different light after they've had intercourse and to be disappointed in him as a human being.

Obviously, as all these consequences indicate, intercourse isn't something to be taken lightly or casually. It demands much more than a physical response.

CHAPTER · 9

Sex for Yourself

Masturbation has been defined in several different ways, but the one I prefer calls it "a deliberate self-stimulation that results in sexual arousal." Others define it in a much broader way. They regard it as any kind of self-stimulation giving pleasure, a definition so broad it would include rubbing the nose and riding on a roller coaster.

We get our conventional views about masturbation from the Judeo-Christian religious tradition, whose founders believed that sex must be only for the purpose of procreation. Since masturbation doesn't result in pregnancy, organized religions have always been against it.

Attitudes today have changed a great deal, and they continue to do so. Even some churches now grant that sex is something pleasurable in its own right, but it isn't easy to change taboos that have persisted for centuries. An astonishing number of adults, including parents, still think masturbation is bad for you, although they wouldn't be able to tell you exactly why. Freud and his followers at least partly justified their views by asserting, in effect, that masturbation might be all right for young children, when it was part of growing up, but it was childish, immature, and undesirable in older people.

It's hardly surprising, then, that many girls are still influenced by negative attitudes coming from parents, churches, or both, and so they feel guilty about it when they masturbate. That's too bad for them, because they won't get all the pleasure that's possible out of masturbating if they allow ancient taboos to interfere.

The truth is that masturbation is only a part of ordinary sexual activity, like fondling or intercourse. There's no more reason to feel guilty about it than about anything else you do sexually, as a human being. Doing it only becomes a problem if a girl's own code or her religion have convinced her that sex is only for procreation and consequently it's morally wrong to masturbate. Or perhaps she may feel that if parents or other respected adults are against it, she ought to conform. I'm sure that doesn't happen often to teenagers. If a girl *does* keep on masturbating even if she has strong moral feelings against it, it may possibly do her more harm than good, in a strictly psychological sense.

Some people, even doctors, have argued that masturbating is harmful because it fixates a girl on that level and makes it difficult or impossible for her to enjoy intercourse. There's no truth in this argument, as I said earlier. Studies show that girls who learn to have orgasm through masturbation have an *easier* time in responding to intercourse than those who don't. In the past there have been wild assertions that masturbation does all kinds of physical harm to young girls (they said the same thing about boys), but there's no truth in that, either. I don't think anyone now believes that masturbating causes pimples, poor posture, dullness of mind, cancer, stomach upsets, sterility, headaches, or kidney trouble. No medical evidence exists showing any kind of relationship between masturbating and illness.

If there's physical harm at all in masturbating, it's an occasional local irritation caused by a great deal of friction, or an even more infrequent minor infection caused by inserting some unclean object into the vagina or urethra.

On the other hand, there are many reasons why masturbation is beneficial. First, it brings a girl much pleasure, especially if she masturbates to orgasm. Stopping short of it may leave her momentarily frustrated and uneasy, with a good deal of congestion in her genitals. That will no doubt be uncomfortable, but it's nothing to worry about.

Masturbation also teaches a girl how to have an orgasm, in the most simple and direct way possible, so it will be easier for her to have one when she *does* have intercourse. Another good reason for masturbating is the fact that it's so easily available. All you need is privacy. Doing it permits a girl to learn how her own body reacts, and allows her to experiment with herself so that she can more easily teach someone else the things that make her feel good sexually. There's no danger of venereal disease or of pregnancy, and masturbation does no harm to a girl or anyone else. It offers a variety of sexual experiences and provides a way to develop a fantasy life, an important part of human sexuality.

Masturbation, however, is another thing that sharply separates boys and girls. Kinsey's figures showed that by the age of fifteen, about 25 percent of girls had masturbated to the point of orgasm, while the figure for boys was virtually 100 percent. No doubt the figure for girls would have to be revised upward today, with greater knowledge and more sexual freedom as well as the impetus of the women's movement.

Eventually more than 60 percent of women masturbate (perhaps even a larger number now), but much of it occurs in later life, even in marriage or some other relationship. For young girls, the average frequency of masturbation was about every two weeks, according to Kinsey's early figures, but that frequency may well have increased, too. In any case, there's a great deal of variation. Some girls do it many times a week, others very infrequently.

Most boys learn how to masturbate by hearing about it from other boys, but most girls discover it for themselves. Again, this reflects the fact that boys do much more talking about sex among themselves than girls do. If the figures are still correct, as many as a quarter of the girls who don't begin masturbating until they're in their early twenties or older still discover it by themselves. Oddly enough, some girls masturbate for a long time before they realize that's what they're doing.

Girls also learn about masturbating from books like this one, or other books, or from other girls, or boys. Less than half the girls learn about it that way, but it's how three-fourths of the boys find out. About one girl in every ten learns of masturbating as the result of being fondled by a boy, and approximately the same number through seeing someone else do it. Only about 3 percent of girls learn from an experience with another girl, but this figure is much higher for boys. Surprisingly, there are still girls who don't know it's possible to masturbate.

However it's learned, the techniques are the same. They center on stimulation of the clitoris, and most girls masturbate by rubbing it or the part of the vulva immediately around it. While there are many different techniques, a girl usually moves a finger or several fingers, or perhaps her whole hand, gently and rhythmically over this section, sometimes supplying steady and increased pressure as she builds toward orgasm. She may also use the heel of her foot or some other object placed against the area. For some girls, only a gentle pressure is needed. Others need to apply so much pressure that it takes one hand on top of another to accomplish it.

This way of masturbating is usually done while a

girl is lying on her back or perhaps sitting up, but it's also done while lying on the stomach, with one hand underneath placed over the vulva and a finger manipulating the clitoris. Some girls like to lie on their stomachs and place a bunched-up sheet or blanket between their legs, rubbing against it to attain orgasm. Others like to rub themselves against objects—stuffed animals, for instance, that they take to bed, or furniture in the room, like the arm of a chair.

Girls are lucky. There are a great many more ways for them to masturbate than boys enjoy. Some girls like to do it in the bathtub, using the stream from a faucet or a needle shower directed against the clitoris. Others do it by crossing their legs and exerting a steady and rhythmic pressure on the whole genital area. The advantage of this method is that it can be done in airplanes, buses, or other public conveyances, or in the classroom, or virtually anywhere else. A girl can swing her crossed legs to cause the pressure, or she can do it even less noticeably by rhythmically tightening and relaxing her thigh muscles. It can also be done by lying facedown, with buttocks moving rhythmically against each other, and with legs either crossed or uncrossed. Whether a girl puts something beneath her when she uses this method—a pillow or part of the bedclothes—doesn't matter, since it isn't the stimulation of something pressing against the sex organ that brings her to orgasm, but the muscular tension in her body, like that developed in the motions of intercourse.

Other ways of building up this muscular tension

include climbing up a pole or a rope, or even chinning on parallel bars. About 50 percent of women also discover that their breasts are erotically sensitive. Approximately one girl in ten stimulates her breast with one hand while she rubs her clitoris with the other. Few girls, however, can achieve orgasm by breast stimulation alone.

About 20 percent of girls insert something in their vaginas to masturbate, but not many do this regularly. The most common object inserted is one or more fingers. When she does that, a girl pulls her hand up against the top of the organ so that the clitoris and the labia minora are stimulated at the same time. A few girls get more satisfaction out of deep vaginal penetration than they do from stimulating the clitoris, but the number is small.

Most boys believe that inserting something is the way girls masturbate, because they think only in terms of the penis being inserted into the vagina. It's hard for them to understand that the girl's area of erotic stimulation is her clitoris, not the vagina.

A variety of other techniques are available, including the use of a vibrator to stimulate the clitoris and the area around it, or using fruits or vegetables (bananas and cucumbers are the most popular) to penetrate the vagina. Some insert objects into the anus. Vibrators are a very effective way for girls to achieve orgasm, and this method is becoming much more common. There's no danger of getting "hooked" on it, as some people mistakenly believe, so that a girl can't achieve an orgasm any other way.

About 2 percent of girls are able to have orgasm by means of conscious fantasy alone. Only one boy in a thousand is able to do this.

If no attempt is made to delay the speed of orgasm, the average girl has a climax in less than four minutes, although some do it in only a few seconds. In intercourse, as we've seen earlier, males often have some trouble holding back their orgasms until a girl is ready, and I've advised boys to learn how to delay it. They can practice doing that in masturbation, and for the same reason it's good for girls *not* to delay orgasm when they masturbate, even if they find they can go on and on and have two or more orgasms in succession.

When boys begin to masturbate, about the time they enter puberty, they tend to keep on doing it regularly until some other kind of sexual activity begins. But even after they get around to fondling girls and having intercourse, they continue to masturbate regularly, although with decreasing frequency.

Girls, however, tend to be much less regular about their masturbation. They may do it a great deal for a period of time, maybe as often as twenty times a week or once a day for two months. Then they'll suddenly stop for a longer period of time. The stopping can be the result of guilt feelings, but more often it simply results from a lack of interest. For quite a few girls there seems to be an absence of sexual desire, with no pressure building up because of a lack of sexual activity, as there is with boys, so that an orgasmic explosion has to occur. That's why girls find it hard to understand this kind of pressure in boys. Similarly, boys find t incomprehensible that girls can take sex or leave it alone so easily.

Another difference between the sexes is what girls think about while they masturbate. A third don't appear to think of anything except the sensation itself. If a girl fantasizes at all, she usually thinks only of sexual experiences she's already had. For example, a girl who has only kissed a boy and never gone further will usually fantasize kissing when she masturbates. A boy in the same situation will probably think of intercourse. Girls tend to fantasize about more general things, like living with a boy, or lying down with him, or being in some romantic setting. Boys are much more specific. They develop scenarios of sexual activity, and the genitals are almost always involved in their fantasies.

Girls who don't have specific sexual fantasies sometimes find them disturbing when they do occur. They might think about having intercourse with a teacher, or with their father or brother, or they imagine they're prostitutes, or that they're being raped. The only harm in such fantasies is a feeling of guilt. Like other daydreams, sex fantasies are part of normal living and should be regarded that way.

Boys have even more elaborate fantasies. Not only do they sometimes imagine having sex with a teacher, or their sister, or their mother or father, but they may imagine an orgy with several girls and boys, or perhaps only boys. They may think, too, of having sex with a particular girl or boy or a grown man or woman, of forcing someone else to have sex, or of being forced themselves.

There's nothing wrong with fantasies about forcing, although it would be very wrong if the fantasies were ever carried out. I've never known a woman who consciously wanted to be raped, and certainly women would resist it in real life if resistance was possible, yet rape fantasies are quite common among girls and women.

Obviously boys have a more elaborate fantasy life than girls. That's only natural because they're more preoccupied with sex. In either sex, chances are small that any of these masturbation fantasies will ever be carried out. They simply add to the excitement, often because what's being fantasized is forbidden. When girls or boys come back to the real world after masturbating and stop fantasizing, they're as much able to deal with reality as ever, and no harm is done.

Both girls and boys sometimes masturbate because of a conflict in their lives that isn't sexual. Boredom, frustration, and loneliness are other motivations. Sometimes they do it because they have a poor opinion of themselves and think they can't make sexual contacts with others. They don't know how to get along with the other sex, or they find themselves in constant conflict with parents.

If they're under great pressure in school, boys particularly tend to masturbate more. It's true that masturbation temporarily relieves tension, whatever its cause, but if the primary reason for masturbating is nonsexual, a girl (or a boy) needs to get some counseling help and try to solve the problems.

One source of sexual feeling I haven't covered unil now is the activity resulting from sexual dreams. This is far more prevalent among boys than girls. Few teen-age girls have orgasm when they're asleep, although it's not uncommon in older women (nearly half of them do), but the percentage among teen-agers is small. The sexual dreams girls have are about the same as the fantasies they have when they masturbate, and the same differences in the content of girls' and boys' dreams exist as in fantasy.

In our complicated society, both girls and boys learn early that people differ in their attitudes about masturbation. Parents, either directly or by their unspoken attitudes, may let them know they believe it's wrong or harmful to their health, or both. Then too, as I've said, if a girl is brought up in a strong religious faith, she gets the same message and in addition the belief that it distracts people from the true purpose of sexuality, marriage, and reproduction. Even if the adults a girl knows don't take any of these attitudes, they often still shrink from encouraging masturbation by calling it something positive and good.

It's no wonder that girls or women, as any sex therapist can testify, will discuss almost any aspect of their sex lives readily until it comes to masturbation. With few exceptions, that's the last thing they'll admit doing, although the new climate of openness about sexuality is changing that reluctance, too.

If they don't discover it for themselves, young girls and boys need to know that masturbation is not only harmless but positively good and healthy, and it should be encouraged because it helps young people grow up sexually in a natural way. More and more people are coming to understand and accept this simple fact.

As we grow up, however, we all learn what's acceptable public behavior and what's done only in private. We learn quickly that masturbation is private. But we should also understand that because something is private doesn't mean it's bad or inferior or "dirty." Masturbating in private is a completely acceptable way of releasing sexual tension, and it's also an important part of growing up. It isn't a substitute for anything else—it's an end in itself. Fear, anxiety, and guilt are the only harmful things that can result from it. Once these are conquered, masturbation is a happy and useful experience.

CHAPTER · 10

What Being Gay Is All About

Homosexual behavior—what we've come to call "being gay"—is sexual behavior between people of the same sex, as I'm sure you know. To understand it better, though, you need to remember that for behavior to be sexual, it has to involve something more than just physical contact. It must result in some change in the body—deeper breathing, a warm skin, a rapid pulse, or some other symptom that can be identified as sexual. By this measurement, two girls walking arm in arm, or with their arms around each other, or kissing, aren't necessarily involved in homosexual behavior, although they could be if they have sexual feelings for each other while they're doing it.

Let's define homosexual behavior more exactly. A woman who has sexual relations with another woman, or who is aroused sexually by one, is known as a lesbian. The word comes from the Greek Islands of Lesbos, where in ancient times the poet Sappho lived and wrote of the joys of lesbian love in glowing verse that has become part of classical literature.

When many people consider the subject of homosexuality, they're confused by thinking of it as something separate and distinct from heterosexuality, which means sexual relations or attraction between members of opposite sexes. Because a girl is sexually aroused by another girl, or even has relations with her, doesn't mean she can't have relations with boys. Girls who like ice cream may also like pie. If a girl is exclusively heterosexual, it means that she's never had any sexual contact with another girl or been aroused by one. She can also be exclusively *homosexual.* Probably 2 to 3 percent of girls fall into that category. About a quarter fall between the two extremes, having some combination of heterosexual and homosexual behavior in their lives. Such girls or women are called bisexuals. I should add that the same categories apply to boys.

It's a common experience for a girl growing up to become very fond of another girl and have warm, affectionate feelings toward her. Your grandmother called it "having a crush." Sometimes it's hard to draw the line between this situation and a sexual feeling.

I'm thinking now of fourteen-year-old Jane, who is constantly in the company of her girl friend Betty.

They spend hours together, talking abut their experiences, their plans for the future, other girls, school, and the thousand things all girls find to talk about. They often put their arms around each other, and if they're separated during summer vacations, they think about each other's company. This is a typical picture of an attraction between girls, of the kind millions have known. Most girls experience it to one degree or another.

Up to this point, there's nothing homosexual in such behavior. But suppose that one night, while Jane is sleeping over with Betty at her house, they embrace each other in their customary warm, affectionate way, and something happens that hasn't happened before. Sexual feelings are aroused. They begin to stroke each other's bodies, especially their breasts and sex organs, and experience sexual excitement from the contact. They may or may not have an orgasm as a result of their sex play, but it's exactly at this point that a warm, ordinary relationship turns into a homosexual response.

Many girls who aren't lesbians have had that kind of experience. Their response was no more than a sexual extension of their past relationship. It may have happened only once or have been repeated infrequently. But there are some girls with strong feelings for other girls, sexually and emotionally, who may become so absorbed in their sexual relationship that they exclude physical and social contact with boys. That may turn out to be their life preference. Not all girls who become lesbians ignore boys, however.

Many have warm and enduring friendships, even sexual relationships, with the opposite sex throughout their lives.

Clearly it isn't just sexual behavior with someone of the same sex that indicates a girl is a lesbian. What appears to be the determining factor is the amount and intensity of the time she spends relating sexually and in other ways with members of the same sex.

The important thing, in my view, is that girls approach whatever sexual preference seems right for them in a positive way and not for negative reasons. If a girl relates to other girls because she's afraid of boys, or because she wants to avoid going out with them so she won't have to face the problems they may bring, the development of her homosexual life will be taking place for the wrong reasons. It's equally true, however, that if she deliberately relates to boys because she's afraid of what others will say about her as a lesbian, the development of her heterosexual life will be equally wrong. All relationships, whether sexual or nonsexual, can be sound only if they're based on positive foundations.

As I told you at the beginning, my major reason for writing this book is to give young women information on human sexuality so they can make informed and intelligent choices on many levels. You'll agree, I'm sure, that any life choice we make is extremely important. So girls who feel a strong pull to lesbianism, to heterosexuality, or to bisexuality need to know all the pros and cons of each. Only that way can they feel in the end that their choice has been made freely, knowingly, and positively—a choice made because it's the way of life they really prefer.

Few people, unfortunately, are able to accept the fact that everyone is *potentially* capable of doing every act imaginable, including having homosexual relations, given the proper circumstances, conditioning, and background. Everyone has homosexual tendencies to one degree or another, but that doesn't mean we'll ever actually *do* anything about it or even be aware of it.

It's a common experience, in fact, to be stirred by a sexual feeling toward someone of the same sex. It may come through a fantasy, a dream, or in some other way. This is an idea that horrifies most people, however. If they have such a conscious thought, they feel instantly guilty about their "perverted" feelings. Yet most people never take part in a homosexual act, and their momentary thoughts or feelings never interfere with their heterosexual lives. Guilt and fear will plague them only if they permit it.

Nevertheless girls are curious about lesbianism when they hear of it. They're both repelled and fascinated. Often they ask, "But what do they *do?*" It may surprise them to know that "they" do what boys and girls do together, except that they don't have intercourse with a penis involved. Sometimes the sexual contact is no more than kissing or tongue kissing, but it usually includes stroking the body and breasts, mutual masturbation, mouths on each other's sex organs, or lying together with sex organs against each other, going through the movements of intercourse. They can vary their lovemaking as much as or more than heterosexual couples.

Only about one girl in ten ever has specific homosexual contacts. Nearly twice that number are aroused psychologically in a specific sexual way by other girls. For girls who have actual contact, the experience is about once in five weeks, on the average. These experiences usually occur in clusters instead of being spread out evenly—the same pattern as in masturbation.

For various complicated reasons there is more tolerance for female homosexuals in our country than for males, although a homosexual act between two females is just as illegal in some states as it is for males. But women are rarely arrested for such behavior and are much less often convicted, except in the armed forces. The reverse is true in some other parts of the world.

Why is this so? Mostly, once more, as a result of our Judeo-Christian ancestors, who regarded women as little more than property. Female sexual behavior that didn't affect males directly was of little concern to lawmakers. Women's masturbation and homosexuality were virtually ignored. Since homosexuality was identified with anal intercourse, the preferred method among male homosexuals, female homosexuality was not considered wrong.

In our own time, female homosexuals attracted little public attention until the Gay Rights movement, involving both sexes, made it clear that women as well as men were emerging from the more or less secret world they had been inhabiting and were demanding to be treated equally with heterosexuals.

Girls are generally more tolerant of homosexual behavior among members of their own sex than boys are of male gays. But girls are quick to condemn or reject other girls who don't do things the way *they* do, or as the group does. That applies to sexual behavior as well as other matters. Girls who wear a different kind of clothing from the currently approved "uniform" or who act in a different way are often ostracized and rejected by the others. Everyone has to conform to whatever the group approves of or else face being shut out.

Fear is one of the chief reasons we reject other people. We're afraid of them because they're not like us and we don't know what they might do. Another is ignorance of their behavior. One of the things I hope to do in this book is to give girls enough information about homosexuality so that at least some of the fear and ignorance will be diminished, and rejection of other people won't be so automatic and unthinking. I believe people should be accepted or rejected solely on the basis of what they are as individuals, rather than whether they like ice cream better than pie.

A few lesbians develop mannerisms like men, both in their dress and in their actions, and may call themselves "butch" or "dykes." Most people have the mistaken idea that this is what all lesbians are like, or that one in each couple is manlike. In reality, only about 5 percent of girls with active homosexual lives develop these characteristics. The same is true of gay men, only a relatively small percentage of whom are effeminate.

We call some girls "tomboys" and sometimes think they're potential lesbians, but they usually have no homosexual inclinations at all. In a great majority of cases it's impossible for a girl to tell whether or not her friends or acquaintances are engaged in homosexual behavior. About 15 percent of homosexual boys are obviously so, which means that a girl in most cases won't be able to tell among the boys she knows which ones are involved in homosexual behavior.

Heterosexuals think that homosexuals have to play the same sex roles they do—that is, one is dominant (male) and the other is submissive (female). Many believe this even though that concept is beginning to disappear in their own lives. While it's true that there are some homosexual relationships constructed on that basis, the great majority of lesbians love each other without playing any role at all.

You've seen girls who like to dress like boys or as nearly so as they can. There are a few others who dress like males, want to *become* males, and think they were meant to be males. In some cases they even have operations to remove their breasts and have rudimentary penises sewn to their bodies so they can perform as males. These people are called "transsexuals." Most girls will probably never meet such a person. They're much more likely to see males who want to become females, and certainly they'll read about the more celebrated of these cases in the newspapers. Several thousand men have been operated on successfully to accomplish this transformation. One of those who did was the noted British writer James Morris, who concluded that he was really female and had a sex change operation. He went on to establish a new reputation as a female writer named Jan Morris. These operations are compromises, in a physical and sexual sense, but psychologically they relieve the intense pressures that led to the change.

As I observed earlier, girls sometimes find themselves having an overwhelming interest in another girl or woman, especially a teacher. They find it extremely flattering to have an older woman take a special interest in them. Many girls have had this experience to one degree or another. These relationships can be happy and helpful ones to a girl growing up, and they rarely lead to sexual activity as parents or other adults may fear.

If sex does become the aim of the older woman, whether or not she's a teacher, the situation is quite different than in the case of an older man making a sexual approach. The older woman's approach is almost sure to be more gradual and gentle, and may never become any more than just that—an approach.

It's also easier for a girl to say no to an older woman than to put off an older man. If she's confronted with this problem, the girl should ask herself the same question she did about the man: Why does this older person want to be involved with a young girl?

Finally, I want to emphasize that homosexual relationships can be as pleasurable, as deep, and as worthwhile as heterosexual ones, even though society still has strong feelings against them. But because there are so many variables to consider and so many nonsexual factors involved, girls ought to be very sure of themselves and how they really feel about their sexual preference before they make such an important decision about how their lives will be lived.

CHAPTER · 11

"... I Forgot to Ask"

Girls who haven't found answers to all their questions in the preceding pages will find them here, I hope. These are questions that have actually been asked by several different groups of young girls. You may not find your own special question, because obviously it would be impossible to set down the hundreds that might be asked. If you still have questions, seek out the answers from a competent authority. It's better to *know* than to wonder and imagine.

1. *Do boys have a different interest in sex than girls, and a different ability to perform sexually?*

I've already answered the first part of this question in some detail, but let me add that there are boys, like some girls, who are "late bloomers" in the sense that they're not really interested in sex until their late teens. After that they have an active sex life.

I had one patient, a boy of twenty-four, who had never experienced an erection in his life because his body was deficient in male hormones. On the other side of the coin, there are boys who seem interested in sex almost from the time they're born. They learn masturbation to orgasm quickly and may do it several times a day. Sometimes they continue an active sexual life until they're old men. Most boys come somewhere between these extremes.

If an individual, either boy or girl, is a highly sexed person, there isn't much that can be done to decrease his or her activity, even if anyone wanted to do it. But if you're at the low end of the scale, it's also true that there isn't much you can do about that, either. People don't have much choice but to accept their level of sexuality, whatever it is.

2. *How long can sperm live?*

They can live in the vagina from one to two days. Under special conditions, some have been kept alive for eight days or more. If sperm are not in a warm, moist, alkaline place, they die quickly.

3. *What is circumcision?*

Girls are often curious about this, especially if they've had a chance to see the different appearance of a penis after this operation has been performed. There is a loose piece of skin extending to the end or beyond the end of the penis known as the "foreskin." The removal of the foreskin is called circumcision. Some think it is done because it is easier to keep the head of the penis and the part just behind it cleaner if the skin is eliminated. All Jewish males are circumcised as a part of their religion.

Sometimes the foreskin sticks to the head of the penis, and a circumcision is necessary to get it unstuck. Sometimes the foreskin has such a small opening that the head of the penis can't be pushed through. That's called "phimosis." If a boy has that condition, it's possible to stretch the foreskin without circumcision. It can be done by inserting the tips of the forefinger of each hand into the opening of the foreskin and stretching it outward for about ten minutes every day. In two weeks or so, the skin will be stretched enough so the penis can emerge freely from it.

There's a white, cheeselike substance called "smegma" that forms behind the head of the penis in uncircumcised males that needs to be washed away every day because it has an unpleasant odor. A girl who smells this shouldn't conclude that a boy has a venereal disease; he just has bad personal hygiene. Nor is there any truth in the popular myth that circumcised males are better lovers or have any other advantages. Unless she's seen the boy's penis before they have intercourse, a girl won't know the difference.

4. *Why is it that if girls sleep around, they're called sluts, but if boys do it, they come off as eligible bachelors, or studs, or playboys?*

That's because of the double standard that's always prevailed—even now. In your grandfather's time, people talked about a boy "sowing his wild oats," and it was winked at unless his conduct became scandalous and public. Girls were expected to be plaster saints. While that idea is not nearly so widely accepted today as a result of the women's movement and changing times, the double standard is not dead, although it varies from one part of society to another and even from one region to another. But thankfully it seems to be slowly disappearing. Boys and girls should be equally responsible for what they do or don't do.

5. *What is "stone ache," or "lover's nuts"?*

In the chapter on orgasm I explained that girls may get an ache in the groin because they have been fondled almost to the point of orgasm, or have masturbated themselves to that point without doing it, so that sexual tension is unrelieved.

This also happens to boys. They, too, get aches in the groin when they've been fondling a girl for a long time, with erection but no orgasm. Because these aches are in their testicles, boys call this condition by the slang terms above. In both sexes the cause is congestion leading to muscle contraction, and the aching of these contracted muscles causes pain. It isn't serious and can be quickly relieved by masturbation.

6. *What is impotence?*

It's something girls don't have to worry about, but it's a serious problem where their sexual partners are concerned. The most common kind is erectile impotence, in which the male can't get an erection. It might happen to a young boy if he's frightened or if he thinks he might not be able to get one. Ejaculatory impotence is less common. That happens when a male can get an erection but is unable to ejaculate. Impotence is usually caused by anxiety and disappears when the causes are removed.

7. *What are other common words for the penis?*

Girls may hear at least some of a long list of synonyms. Some of them are "cock," "dick," "prick," "peter," "pecker," "dong," or—left over from childhood—"wee-wee."

8. *What are other words for testicles?*

Again, knowing what these words are may clear up a few mysterious references girls hear in conversation or read in books. The two most common synonyms are "balls" and "nuts," but there are many others. Girls today are much more likely to be familiar with all

these words, since they appear so commonly in print
and have even become a part of common speech.

9. *What are other names for masturbation?*

One or two are used by both sexes, such as "playing with yourself." Girls sometimes say "rubbing off."
Most of the others are used by boys—words like "jack-
ing off," "jerking off," "beating your meat," or simply,
"getting it off." The latter phrase is common today,
but it also has other meanings.

10. *What are other words for sexual intercourse?*

Here again times are changing. Until recently "co-
itus" and "copulation" were the medical terms used in
polite society and in the media. American newspapers
have never gotten much beyond them. But in everyday
speech there are literally hundreds of them, and some
are the most common words in the English language.
It's been said jokingly that the Second World War, let
alone Korea and Vietnam, could not have been fought
without the words "fuck" and "fucking." We still don't
see these words in our newspapers or hear them on
television, but movie dialogue using these words is
now commonplace, and for some time they've appeared freely in books, much less so in magazines.
"Screw" is almost as common, often used as a substitute by those who can't bring themselves to say the
other word. Other euphemisms are "lay," "sleep

with," (the most common), the old-time word "jel-lyroll," an early part of black slang, and in that same category, "poontang" and "jazz." These words vary from region to region, and from one social level to another.

11. *Are there times when a girl either doesn't want or can't have intercourse?*

The times when a girl *wants* intercourse vary greatly from girl to girl, but on the average, girls are more easily aroused on the day or two before they menstruate and a little less so on the day or two following menstruation. A third likely time is during the menstrual period. This isn't true for every girl, however. Some don't vary much in their sexual feelings from one day or week to the next.

While there's no harm in having intercourse with a girl who's menstruating, as I've said, many of them don't want to have it then because they have cramps, or because they think it's too messy, or because of social taboos. This is especially true of those who are Orthodox Jews and follow the fundamentalist teaching that intercourse during menstruation is unclean and wrong.

When they feel like having sex, girls are usually reacting more to the mood or the occasion. Naturally if they've just had a quarrel with a boy, or if they're feeling upset about something, or if the time and place just don't seem right to them, they're not likely to want to be handled, much less have intercourse. Occasionally there may be medical reasons why a girl shouldn't have intercourse, especially if she has an infection in her vagina or urethra.

12. *Do particular foods or drugs stimulate the sex drive?*

The answer is no. If a girl wants to stimulate her sex drive (and not many would think of doing it), she should get plenty of sleep, eat nourishing food, and keep herself in general good health.

There are a good many old wives' tales about this subject. One is the superstition that foods like raw oysters, eggs, or malted milk (among other substances) stimulate sexual interest. There's no truth in this or any related idea. A particular word of caution: A girl should never permit a boy, or permit herself, to use the powdered drug known as "Spanish fly" or cantharides. It's commonly believed that the application of this drug will make the female extremely excited sexually. What it actually does is to irritate the lining of the urethra, and if taken in sufficient quantity, it's highly poisonous. It has no effect on sexuality. For centuries people have tried to find medicines or drugs to help stimulate them or their partners sexually— what we call "aphrodisiacs." But nothing has ever been found that will do it except the injection of male hormones in men, and that may have dangerous side effects.

13. *What is a pimp?*

A pimp is a man who manages a prostitute and takes a part or all of her earnings. In effect, he's her business manager, but he's also likely to think of her as his property. Occasionally he may get customers for her, but he usually leaves that up to her. In common usage, however, "to pimp" is used in a nonsexual sense, meaning to get something illegally for someone else. It is also sometimes used as a general term of contempt for a man who's weak, shifty, or worthless.

14. *What is a male prostitute?*

A man who has sexual relations with another man for money. In male prostitution, the customer pays for the privilege of having the prostitute ejaculate. There are also a few male prostitutes who are paid by women.

15. *What is a hermaphrodite?*

A true hermaphrodite is one who has the testicles and ovaries of both sexes. Few such individuals exist, but there are pseudohermaphrodites who are anatomically somewhere between the two sexes—for example, a boy with a tiny penis, like a clitoris, or a girl with a clitoris almost large enough to be a penis. Corrective surgery can often make such a person more like a conventional male or female. Other pseudohermaphrodites may be a man who has large breasts like a woman's, a woman with no breasts at all, or a woman with hair on her face, like a man—the "bearded woman" of the circus and the carnival sideshow. These people aren't really hermaphrodites. Usually their problem is a hormone imbalance. People often use corruptions of the word, like "amorphodite," or "morphadite," because they don't know the correct word.

16. *What is castration?*

Castration means removal of the testicles of males, or removal of the ovaries of the female. Since these are the main source of male hormones for the boy, an adolescent boy who has been castrated will have no growth of hair on his face. The remainder of his body hair will become fine and silky, while his voice remains high like that of a preadolescent. He can't ejaculate and often can't get an erection. Such people are called "eunuchs," (pronounced *yew-nuk*). The older a man is, the less effect there'll be if he's castrated. The equivalent operation in females, also called castration, is removal of the ovaries, which makes them unable to have children although it does not produce the same side effects as in males.

17. *What is abnormal sex?*

I can't really answer this question, even though the phrase is used so much, because the word "abnormal" is ambiguous. Let me explain that a little more. It can mean something unusual or rare, so by that definition it is abnormal to have intercourse by hanging from the chandelier—to take a really far-out example—because few if any people have intercourse in such a position. Using that definition, however, masturbation has to be considered normal (as it is) because most boys and girls masturbate; homosexuality, too, is almost normal because so many are involved in it.

Another way of defining "abnormal" is to say it's anything unnatural. Since human sexual behavior is like that of other animals, it has to be considered natural. All mammals, of which humans are a species, engage in practically every kind of sex, so by this definition there is essentially nothing that humans do sexually that can be called abnormal.

A third way to look at "abnormal" is through the eyes of society. Our laws and churches are the guide here, although they're not always in complete agreement. In fact, some churches today are much more liberal than they used to be. For example, it isn't against the law to masturbate, except in public, but some religious people think it's wrong. On the other hand, it's against the law in about half the states to put your mouth on the sex organ of another person. Many religious leaders don't believe this is wrong, and many husbands and wives, as well as other people, do it.

Still another way to think about "abnormal" is to consider what sexual acts harm other people. That would include forcing other people to engage in sexual behavior against their will, or lying to them, cheating them, or seducing them in order to get them to do what they don't want to do. All these could be considered abnormal.

It's easy to see what a complicated business it is to try to decide what's abnormal sex. That's why I'm suggesting the question can't be given a definite, clear-cut answer.

18. *What is a wet dream?*

This is something that happens more often to boys, but girls can experience it as well, as I noted in the chapter on masturbation. A boy may wake up some night or in the morning to discover that he's had an ejaculation while he was asleep. Some boys may be alarmed by this if they've heard the myth that loss of semen during sleep is somehow damaging. A "wet dream" is simply the result of sexual excitement caused by dreaming, which eventually reaches a climax with the emission of semen. It isn't an automatic substitute for intercourse, as some think, or even a means of relieving sexual tension; in fact, it may even follow sexual intercourse. It occurs much less often with girls, as I've said, but they too can be aroused to the point of orgasm by what they're dreaming.

19. *What is adultery, and what is fornication?*

People sometimes mix up the meanings of these words. Adultery is sexual experience when one or both persons are married, but not to each other. Fornication is intercourse when neither partner is married. These are legal terms. In every state, adultery is against the law, and in about half of them fornication is also illegal.

20. *Are necrophilia and bestiality moral or immoral?*

First, I'd better explain what they are for those who might not know. Necrophilia is having sex with a dead person; bestiality is having it with an animal. Necrophilia is considered immoral by nearly everyone, and it's a crime besides. It is a rare sexual aberration.

Bestiality, however, is a somewhat different matter. Technically, intercourse with animals is called "bestiality." While most people think it's immoral, at the least, and repulsive as well, it's practiced around the globe and has been known as far back as the ancient world. About 2 percent of city and nearly 20 percent of farmboys in the Kinsey survey reported having had sexual experience with animals. About 2 percent of both farm and city girls reported having had it. As to whether it's immoral or not, that depends entirely on the point of view.

21. *What is sadomasochism?*

The word is a contraction of two others—"sadism," meaning to get sexual pleasure from giving pain to someone else, and "masochism," meaning to get sexual pleasure from pain inflicted by someone else—in both cases, with mutual consent. The words are combined because most people who get sexual pleasure from hurting others also get it from being hurt. These words are often used in a nonsexual (and incorrect) way, defining a sadist as someone who enjoys hurting other people, and a masochist as one who appears to get satisfaction out of being humiliated.

There's a little sadomasochism in all of us. For example, people who are aroused sexually often enjoy nibbling, biting, or scratching. Others develop much stronger behavior patterns in this direction. They enjoy being beaten, whipped, tied down, or given similar treatment. Boys and girls sometimes think of such activity when they masturbate, or at other times. There's no cause to worry about such thoughts.

22. *What is incest?*

In a legal sense, incest means having sexual intercourse with a relative of the opposite sex. It could be mother, father, brother, sister, grandparent, or grandchild. In some states, this list would include uncles, aunts, and first cousins, and usually stepparents, stepchildren, stepbrothers, and stepsisters, even though they're not blood relatives. Adopted children are also included.

In a broader sense, incest doesn't necessarily mean sexual intercourse, but includes any kind of sexual relations, homosexual included, between relatives. In real life, however, sex play with sisters, brothers, and cousins of both sexes is not at all unusual in preadolescence.

Incest is the oldest of all the taboos, going back to

earliest times, and it remains the strongest. Guilt alone is a strong inhibition, and of course all religions absolutely forbid incest. There are also biological reasons for the taboo; at least so it was believed until recently. Some scientists have challenged the theory that children of an incestuous union are likely to inherit the outstanding bad characteristics of both parents. Genetically, it was said, continuing incestuous relationships in a group, so that children resulted, would tend to "breed out"—that is, the bad traits and defects would eventually overcome the good ones in successive generations. Considerable doubt has been shed on these long held beliefs; they remain controversial and inconclusive. Some scientists, however, now think there is no basis for this theory.

Regardless of genetic outcomes, however, it must be noted that incest in families between father and daughter, for instance, can and often does cause serious psychological damage to a child, with sometimes profound long-range consequences.

23. *Should children be allowed to run around the house without any clothes on?*

One of the paradoxes of human life is that we're told constantly and in many ways how beautiful the human body is, yet we're ashamed to show it in front of other people except within certain limits. As a look at swimsuit styles will show, the limit has now been pushed to its farthest extreme.

This need to cover the body is as old as Adam and

Eve, in one sense. People originally covered themselves as protection from the weather, but in time it
became a matter of religion, and in our own society it's
a heritage from the strict religious feelings of the early
colonists, whose Puritanism, as we call it now, set the
tone of American life in its moral aspects. Consequently people can't be as free as some might like to
be, short of joining a nudist colony, because they'll
feel the weight of society's displeasure and its laws.
But people can be more relaxed about nudity in the
privacy of their own homes if their standards are different from those of society.

Parents set these standards, for the most part. To a
large extent they determine how much nudity is permitted, and also where and when. No matter what's
decided, the human body remains beautiful and people should feel no shame in viewing it.

24. *What is a douche?*

I've explained this in Chapter 8: it's a means of
washing out semen from the vagina in order not to
become pregnant—a highly ineffective procedure. But
I should add here that its too frequent use can be
harmful, in the opinion of most doctors, because it
washes out natural lubricating liquids from the vagina.
Unless there's some infection, they advise against it.
Some girls do it as a matter of personal hygiene, but
it's just as effective to use soap and water outside the
sex organ to cleanse the secretions that form, particularly around the clitoris and inner lips.

25. *What is a miscarriage?*

A miscarriage (sometimes called a "spontaneous abortion") is the loss of the fetus before it's able to live outside the mother. Sometimes it's caused by the physical condition of the mother—certain forms of fibroid tumors, tears in the womb mouth from childbirth, or a misshapen uterus. Others result from general illnesses, like abnormal gland function, chronic high blood pressure, uncontrolled diabetes, untreated syphilis, severe undernourishment, and high fevers. Careful medical supervision can forestall miscarriage in diabetics and women with high blood pressure.

These physical causes, however, are involved only in the minority of miscarriages. Most of them result from what is called by doctors "defective germ plasm." Almost three out of four miscarriages are the result of defective eggs. A fetus that develops improperly usually dies and is expelled from the body as foreign material by muscular contractions of the uterus. A defective-germ-plasm conception usually stops developing after six or seven weeks but is carried in the uterus for three or four weeks longer. A miscarriage occurs usually around the tenth or eleventh week of pregnancy.

Contrary to popular belief, few miscarriages are caused by a blow or a jolt or an emotional upheaval. Most doctors agree, as one specialist puts it, "You can't shake a good human egg loose, any more than a fresh wind will cause healthy unripe apples to fall from the tree."

Miscarriage usually offers virtually no risk to a woman, although she may bleed enough to require a transfusion. She should recover in a few days.

26. *What is sodomy?*

The word comes from the Biblical town of Sodom, the sinful city, in which people were supposed to have been involved in "unnatural sex practices." We have no idea what those practices really were. Sodomy sometimes means any homosexual practice, or putting the mouth on the sex organ of another person, whether in homosexual or heterosexual contact. It also includes anal intercourse, whether homosexual or heterosexual, and any sexual contact between humans and other animals. Most states have strict laws against sodomy.

27. *What does the expression "female trouble" mean?*

It refers to any kind of physical complaint a woman might have in connection with her sex organs, including trouble with menstruation, the vagina, ovaries, or uterus. It isn't heard much these days.

28. *What does "caesarean section" mean?*

It means the birth of a baby through the abdominal wall. The uterus is cut open and the baby is taken directly out of it without passing through the vagina.

This is usually done if the baby is too small or in the wrong position, or if the mother has some physical condition that would make regular birth too difficult. In modern medical practice, it isn't a dangerous operation, although it is now argued that it's done more often than is necessary. Many women have perfectly healthy babies delivered by this method.

29. *Does a man ever urinate in a woman during intercourse?*

It's very difficult, though not impossible, for a man to urinate with an erect penis, and it's hard to have intercourse without an erection. Consequently this happens only rarely. It's much easier for a woman to do so in the same circumstances, and occasionally it occurs as part of an intense orgasm.

30. *What does a man do when he rapes a woman?*

With all the current prevalence of rape in the newspapers and other media, and the consequent heightened awareness, you wouldn't think this question would ever be asked, but some young girls don't know, except in a general way.

The word means "to have intercourse by force." There are all kinds of possible force. If a man pins a woman down with his body and struggles with her for a long time until she gives in, and then has intercourse with her against her will, that's rape, whether they're strangers or have some kind of relationship. "Acquaintance rape" seems to be much more frequent these days.

Again, the use of a weapon to threaten a woman into submitting is also rape. According to law a girl who is under a certain age (sixteen in some states, as high as twenty-one in others) is technically unable to give consent. Consequently any intercourse of the kind I've been talking about here is called "statutory rape" even if a girl is willing, or "rape with consent," if she's under the prescribed age.

31. *What is a fetus?*

Any unborn baby. Up to seven weeks, this is also known as an "embryo."

32. *How does artificial insemination work?*

Sometimes a husband can't make his wife pregnant because he hasn't manufactured enough sperm, or because the sperm die before reaching the egg, or for several other reasons, some physical and some psychological. In these cases it's sometimes possible to inject his semen into his wife artificially and she becomes pregnant. In other cases it's necessary to use semen from another man. Semen is placed in the vagina by a doctor; it's an office procedure. If the semen comes from someone else, the woman never sees the donor or knows who he is. It's estimated that about ten thousand or more children are born this way in the United States every year.

33. *What's the difference in pubic hair between boys and girls?*

A girl's is finer and silkier, like the hair on her head, and it's also distributed more in the shape of a triangle, wider at the top. Some boys think they can tell whether the color of a girl's hair is natural if it's the same color as her pubic hair, but the real comparison is with the eyebrows. A blond girl's pubic hair will tend to be darker than her head hair, a brunette's will be lighter. As people get older, pubic hair tends to become gray, although it changes at a much slower rate than head hair.

In boys the hair grows around the penis, especially directly above it. In some boys a line of hair grows up to the navel as they grow older. A few girls also have this line. There is also some pubic hair growing from a boy's scrotum, and even in back of it and around the anus.

A girl's pubic hair doesn't interfere with intercourse because there isn't any on the upper lips of the vulva or on the inside of the outer lips.

34. *How does a hospital determine if a girl has been raped?*

It *can't* tell, in a legal sense, but it *can* determine whether a girl has had intercourse recently if there's still some semen in the vagina. Bruises or scratches, freshly inflicted, may indicate the use of force. If a girl's hymen has been broken by the act, it may still be bleeding, or there will be traces of blood, and that is further evidence. But it would be difficult to determine, in a physical sense, whether rape has been committed or not.

35. *Suppose a girl has intercourse and menstruates some time afterward. Is she pregnant?*

A few girls menstruate a time or two after they become pregnant, but in the great majority of cases it stops when pregnancy begins.

36. *What is menopause?*

Menopause, or "change of life" or "the change," as it's commonly known, should be understood by both girls and boys because their mothers will be experiencing it. Between forty-five and fifty-five, usually, women stop producing an egg cell every month. This isn't a serious loss at that age, especially since menstruation also stops. But the female hormone (estrogen) may also somewhat diminish, and this can produce uncomfortable feelings. Physicians have learned how to treat this normal stage of a woman's life with additional hormones. In any case, once more contrary to popular belief, her sexual life will not change unless she chooses; it will go on exactly as it did before menopause.

37. *Is the size of the penis determined by any other part of the body?*

No. A tall, heavy man can have a short penis, or a short, slight man can have a large one. The average length is about six inches, but there's great variation. In any case, there's no connection between size and sexual activity.

38. *Is it possible for a girl to get pregnant without actually having intercourse?*

No, except in rare circumstances. There's only one chief way, and that's through intercourse, but it can happen if a woman is artificially inseminated, or semen near or in the opening of the vagina enables sperm cells to work their way upward, as described before.

39. *Can you get pregnant if there's semen on a boy's hand and he puts his fingers into the girl?*

Yes. It's not so likely to happen as if the penis were inside the vagina when ejaculation occurs, but if a boy masturbates, let's say, and his hand is covered with sperm, which he immediately transfers with his fingers into the vagina, pregnancy can occur. I should repeat something that I said earlier, however: Sperm cells that don't have the moist, warm vagina to live in, where they might remain alive for hours, die quickly if they remain outside.

40. *What are the chances of getting AIDS from open-mouth kissing?*

No one has calculated the odds because not enough is known, and there is even some disagreement about whether this is possible at all. Most experts agree that the AIDS virus can't be transmitted via saliva. Having oral sex is another matter, however, as I've explained in the text.

41. *Are people weakened by having ejaculations or orgasms?*

No way. On the contrary, the act often has a soothing effect, so that a person who is very tense may feel more relaxed after ejaculation or orgasm. No matter how the orgasm is brought about, whether by masturbation, intercourse, or some other method, what happens to the body is the same physiologically. Of course, society puts different values on these methods. For example, some people are upset by the idea of an aging man getting an ejaculation through masturbation, although the same people probably wouldn't care how often a younger married man ejaculated through intercourse.

Such attitudes are absurd and have nothing to do with reality. If a man's body should reach a physiological point where the amount of sex he has is more than he can handle, he won't be able to have an orgasm until he has rested for a while. The amount of time he'll need depends on his age, physical condition, and some psychological factors.

42. *Does a person have just so much sex to use up in a lifetime, and if you use it up when you're young, will it prevent you from having a sex life when you're older?*

No, the body doesn't work that way. In fact, it seems to operate almost in the opposite fashion. Generally speaking, boys and girls who start having sex the earliest—sex of some kind, that is—are the ones most likely to have the longest active sex lives and to have the most sex when they're older. That doesn't mean, however, that if you start out deliberately to have a lot of sex when you're young that you'll be guaranteed to have a lot when you're older. It means simply that bodies are different from each other. Some people are more highly endowed with the ability to perform sexually throughout their lives.

43. *What's the difference between sex and love?*

They're really separate things. It's possible to have a great deal of affection for parents, your dog, or your best friend without having sex enter the picture. It's also possible to have sex with other people in a hostile, even cruel way without having any affection for them. In most cases, though, love in some degree and sexual feelings are part of the same response to someone else. When these two things occur together, it can be one of the most profound and meaningful experiences it's possible to have.

My own belief is that being "in love" is not something separate and distinct from being "not in love" but is part of a scale—say from zero to a hundred. If you have a boy you like, you're somewhere along the lower end of the scale. But as you get to know him better, go out with him more, and like him even more, you move up the scale until you may experience butterflies in the stomach when you see him and find yourself thinking of him constantly, so you can say positively, "I'm in love." But you may still be a long way from the top of the scale, and as you continue going out with him, you'll find your position probably changes in one direction or another.

It works out better if affection is the beginning of the relationship, with sexual feelings entering the picture later, rather than the other way around. Infatuation, or puppy love, often comes very quickly. Sometimes it happens the first time you see a boy, but it takes a long time, if ever, for that to develop into the kind of love that's based on trust, understanding, consideration, and open communication.

44. *What is a nymphomaniac?*

It was once believed that some women had insatiable sexual appetites and could never be satisfied. The same condition in men was called "satyriasis." Dr. Kinsey exploded this idea in his reports on sexuality in the human male and female by showing that there was the widest possible variation in human sexual activity and there was nothing that could be considered "too much" or "too little." Kinsey himself defined a nymphomaniac as "someone who has more sex than you do."

Afterword

I want to add a word here about sex in relation to a girl's life, since it doesn't exist as something separate and apart from day-to-day living. It's true that sex is very important, but it's unrealistic to overemphasize it. The amount of time a girl spends thinking about sex, even in adolescence, when it all seems new and exciting, usually takes up only a small part of her thoughts. Her actual sexual activity is likely to be even less, unlike an adolescent boy's—and even for him sexual thoughts and activity are going to take up only a relatively small part of a total day.

If a girl masturbates, she probably won't be doing it as often as a boy, and when she goes out with a boy, the sexual part of the evening, if any, may be only a small part of it. As I've said before, girls tend to take a much more romantic view of sex in these early years than boys do. They're already process-oriented, just as the boys are goal-oriented, where sex is concerned.

For anyone, sex is clearly an important part of life, but it's a rather small part of the whole. If girls or boys spend a good part of their waking hours thinking about sex or doing something sexual, it's often because they're upset about it—feeling guilty, or anxious, or unsure. I hope this book will relieve girls of some of those guilt feelings, anxieties, and uncertainties, and that may decrease the amount of time they may spend thinking about sex, or being actively engaged in it.

I'm not suggesting that it's better not to become involved with sex. On the contrary, I believe it's both worthwhile and pleasurable, as I'm sure the contents of this book demonstrate. But if a girl feels guilty or anxious about it, something valuable is lost—something that can make her feel one inch small or ten feet high.

There's one important thing to remember. It isn't what you do sexually that matters, *as long as you're not hurting someone else.* It's how you *feel* about what you're doing. If you learn nothing else from these pages, that fact alone can make the difference between leading a whole life and only part of one.

Both girls and boys discover as they grow up that society tries to restrict what they're allowed to do sexually, but at the same time it constantly stimulates their sexual interest through advertising, clothing, motion pictures, magazines, and television. They find themselves in a world that seems to be preoccupied with sex yet imposes strict prohibitions that remain a threat even though they're violated every day in the week.

You may be surprised to know that your great-grandparents knew something about that situation. In their day, when they were children, everyone knew a familiar rhyme, all but forgotten now. It sounds old-timey, I know, but it represents a social attitude that hasn't changed fundamentally:

> Mother, may I go out to swim?
> Yes, my darling daughter;
> Hang your clothes on a hickory limb,
> And don't go near the water.

I hope this book will teach you how to swim without drowning in a social sea that may not be nearly as angry and restrictive as it was in your grandmother's or even your mother's day, but may be twice as confusing.

For Further Reading

Arnold, Caroline. *Sex Hormones: Why Males and Females Are Different.* New York: Morrow, 1981.

Bell, Ruth, et al. *Changing Bodies, Changing Lives: A Book for Teens on Sex and Relationships.* New York: Random House, 1981.

Eagan, Andrea B. *Why Am I So Miserable If These Are the Best Years of My Life?* New York: Harper, 1976.

Hamilton, Eleanor. *Sex, with Love: A Guide for Young People.* Boston: Beacon Press, 1978.

Hein, Karen, and Theresa Foy DiGeronimo. *AIDS: Trading Fears for Facts.* New York: Consumer Reports Books, 1989.

Hettlinger, Richard. *Growing Up with Sex: A Guide for the Early Teens,* rev. ed. New York: Continuum, 1980.

Hopper, C. Edmund, and William A. Allen. *Sex

   Education for Physically Handicapped Youth.
   Springfield, IL: C.C. Thomas, 1980.

Johnson, Eric. *Love and Sex in Plain Language,* 3rd
   ed. New York: Harper & Row, 1985.

Lena, Dan, and Marie Howard. *Hands Off . . . I'm
   Special! How to Tell Your Boyfriend No.* Hollywood,
   FL: Compact Books, 1987.

McGuire, Paula. *It Won't Happen to Me: Teenagers Talk
   About Pregnancy.* New York: Delacorte Press,
   1983.

Madaras, Lynda. *Lynda Madaras Talks to Teens About
   AIDS: An Essential Guide for Parents, Teachers, and
   Young People.* New York: Newmarket Press, 1988.

Marsh, Carole. *I Con . . . If You Con(dom): The Ins
   and Outs of Contraception for the Sexually Active Girl
   or Boy.* Bath, NC: Gallopade Publishing Group,
   1987.

————. *Sex Stuff for Boys: Sperm, Squirm, and Other
   Squiggly Stuff.* Bath, NC: Gallopade Publishing
   Group, 1987.

————. *Sex Stuff for Girls: A Period Is More Than a
   Punctuation Mark.* Bath, NC: Gallopade
   Publishing Group, 1987.

————. *STD Is Not Motor Oil: The Truth and
   Consequences of Sexually Transmitted Diseases.* Bath,
   NC: Gallopade Publishing Group, 1987.

Sciacca, Fran, and Jill Sciacca. *Sex: When to Say Yes.*
   Dan Mills, ON, Canada: Worldwide, 1987.

Voss, Jacqueline, and Jay Gale. *A Young Woman's
   Guide to Sex.* Los Angeles: Price Stern Sloan,
   1988.

Westheimer, Ruth, and Nathan Kravetz. *First Love: A Young People's Guide to Sexual Information.* New York: Warner Books, 1987.

Wood, Barry. *Questions Teenagers Ask About Dating and Sex.* Old Tappan, NJ: Revell, 1981.

Index